Navajo Rugs

Navajo Rugs

How to Find, Evaluate, Buy and Care for Them

by Don Dedera

with a foreword by Clay Lockett

NORTHLAND PRESS

Frontispiece: *A rare, woman's wearing blanket dating to 1870–75, combines white warp and weft of natural dark and combed gray, indigo, vegetal yellow and a red, possibly cochineal, 42 x 79 inches.* COURTESY SAN DIEGO MUSEUM OF MAN

To Cherie Lee, a weaver at heart.

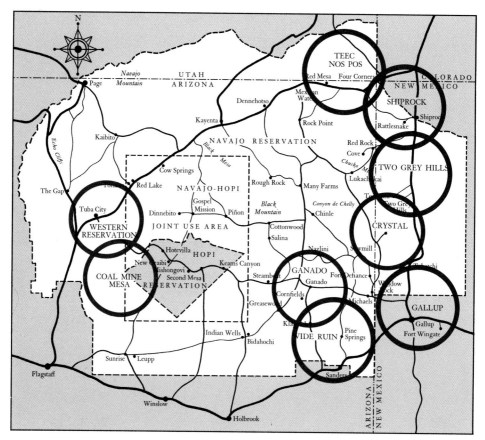

In this map of the Navajo Reservation the names of regional rugs are displayed in circles which designate the general areas where they originated. In previous years those areas were the exclusive sources for the rugs bearing the area name and design, colors, etc. associated with that name. However, in recent years rugs of all styles are woven throughout the Reservation. There are no longer regional rugs, only regional styles.

Contents

Illustrations ix

Foreword xi

CHAPTER 1: The Lords of the Earth 1

CHAPTER 2: How Navajo Women Learn to Weave 7

CHAPTER 3: From Dingy Sheep to Exquisite Rug 15

CHAPTER 4: Pueblo Looms, Spanish Sheep, Navajo Artistry . . 25

CHAPTER 5: The Blanket That Went on the Floor 33

CHAPTER 6: Contemporary is Cosmopolitan 43

CHAPTER 7: Whither Navajo Weaving? 93

CHAPTER 8: A Buyer's Guide to Navajo Weaving 97

CHAPTER 9: Fakes, Frauds and Foolishness 103

CHAPTER 10: The Care and Feeding of a Navajo Weave . . . 107

Acknowledgments 110

Selected Readings 111

Index 112

Illustrations

Frontispiece ii

Map vi

1. Lords of the Earth xiv
2. Navajo medicine man . . . 3
3. Weaver demonstration . . . 8
4. Pueblo style blanket 9
5. Chief blanket, first phase . . 10
6. Chief blanket, second phase . 11
7. Chief blanket, third phase . . 11
8. Massacre Cave dress fragment 13
9. Window Rock, Arizona . . . 14
10. Weaver combing wool . . . 17
11. Spinning of carded wool . . 17
12. Loom sketch 19
13. Shears 20
14. Two types of cards 20
15. Hardwood combs 21
16. Spindle, flywheel and battens 21
17. Re-creation of 19th century
    rug 22
18. Plain weave: detail 23
19. Diamond twill: detail . . . 23
20. Tapestry weave: detail . . . 23
21. Classic serape 24

22. Classic child's shawl 26
23. Poncho style serape 27
24. Serape 28
25. Serape 29
26. Woman's dress 30
27. Germantown serape 32
28. Teec Nos Pos style rug . . . 34
29. Table runner 35
30. *Yeibichai* rug 36
31. "Pound" blanket 37
32. Wedgeweave blanket . . . 38
33. Serape in *moki* pattern . . . 39
34. Rug in a rainbow of
    handspun 39
35. 1911 rug catalog 41
36. Typical red Ganado 42
37. Hubbell Trading Post . . . 45
38. One-of-a-kind rug 47
39. Chief blanket, third phase . 47
40. A Klagetoh 49
41. Modern Crystal 51
42. Two Gray Hills 53
43. Two Gray Hills 55
44. Two Gray Hills 56

45. Two-faced Wide Ruin style   58
46. Pine Springs/Burnt Water
    tapestry   59
47. Two-faced Wide Ruin . . .   60
48. A vegetal-dyed handspun .   61
49. A modern Wide Ruin . . .   61
50. Teec Nos Pos style   62
51. Teec Nos Pos tapestry . . .   63
52. Teec Nos Pos tapestry . . .   64
53. Re-creation from 1911
    catalog   65
54. Storm pattern   66
55. Raised-outline weave . . .   67
56. Gallup throw rug   69
57. Two-faced *yei* rug   70
58. Sandpainting rug   71
59. *Yeibichai* rug   72
60. Double-saddle size twill
    weave   73
61. Twill weave and detail . . .   75
62. Single-saddle blanket . . .   76
63. Double-saddle, tapestry
    weave   77

64. Three examples of "natural"
    weave   78
65. Pictorial rug   80
66. Patriotic pictorial rug . . .   82
67. Pictorial butterfly tapestry .   83
68. Pictorial rug   84
69. Pictorial rug   85
70. "Railroad Blanket," 1892 . .   86
71. Sandpainting rug   89
72. Sandpainting rug   90
73. "The weaver's pathway" . .   91
74. Weaver spinning wool . . .   92
75. Canyon de Chelly   94
76. Navajo Craftsman Show . .   96
77. Helen Kirk   98
78. Grace Henderson Nez . . .   98
79. Yelthdezbah Davis   99
80. Elizabeth Kirk   99
81. Mary Begay   100
82. Betty Shirley   100
83. Mexican *yei* rug: detail . .   102
84. Mexican *yei* rug   104
85. Award-winning Crystal . .   106

Foreword

IN THE LATE TWENTIES when I was studying archaeology in college I soon discovered that I was more interested in live Indians than dead ones. Although my studies exposed me to a lot about Indian culture, religion, social organization and many other aspects of their lives, I was mainly attracted to the things Indians made — the jewelry, pottery, baskets, paintings, but above all others — rugs. I've always felt that a good rug was more beautiful than all other Indian crafts. A rug not only required creativity, but long hours of patient work, and a high level of skill.

I hope I made the point I like rugs best. Years back I read all I could find on rugs, but didn't discover any great rug books. So I haunted museums and hunted up weavers and harassed traders. Before long I had, though not easily, learned an awful lot about rugs, and damned if I didn't begin thinking about writing a book on Navajo rugs. Unexpectedly for Christmas in the early thirties I received a copy of Charles Amsden's new book, *Navajo Weaving*. I didn't even know he was doing it, but he said all the things I had planned to say, and then went ahead and added a bunch of things I certainly didn't even know about. I quickly realized the world sure didn't need a book by me on Navajo rugs.

For many years I was a trader, and over a couple of decades people complained again that there weren't any good, up-to-date books on Navajo weaving. Again, they said I should up-date the Amsden book or write a new one. Well, I began to think about it. I felt what was needed was a book that was accurate but not too technical — a book everyone could benefit from reading easily.

Now, Don Dedera has written an excellent, accurate book that brings Navajo weaving up to the mid-1970s, and again the world is saved from my writing a book on Navajo rugs.

CLAY LOCKETT

Navajo Rugs

The Lords of the Earth

THE NAVAJO. *T'áá diné. The people,* they call themselves.

Self-esteem among societies is not uncommon, yet few of the world's cultures cling so tenaciously as Navajo Indians to the notion that they are a superlative people. Even to objective outsiders this Navajo attitude seems justified. Through long, dismal decades they never lost their pride. Through revolutionary changes in geography, in climate, in economy, in politics, they prevailed as a people, retaining essential Navajo traits.

Today they occupy longtime homelands, keep alive their own tongue, practice a religion based on harmony with nature, honor prehistoric family and clan customs, and exalt beautiful objects of individual creation. And in the latter category, tribal ego is expressed most sensationally in the color, design and refinement of Navajo weaving.

To understand how *diné* persevered as a people, it is helpful to know something of the Navajo past. By physique and language they are related to Asia, by kinship with Athapaskan tribes of western Canada and interior Alaska. By legend, the first Navajos emerged from the underground. Anthropologists believe that as nomadic hunters and gatherers they drifted by small bands from A.D. 1100 to 1500 to settle in that part of the American Southwest now known as Four Corners — where New Mexico, Colorado, Utah and Arizona join.

Here, in the arid, elemental expanses of the high, Colorado Plateau country, Navajo capacities for adaptation were supremely tested. To survive in the land of little water they became farmers, borrowing the techniques of Pueblo neigh-

1. *Lords of the Earth*

PHOTO BY HERB AND DOROTHY MCLAUGHLIN

bors. They took up weaving and sandpainting. They adopted (again, according to anthropologists) Puebloan religion and social structure.

When Spaniards began penetrating the Southwest, Indian villages fell one by one and, except during relatively brief revolts, came under foreign rule. Not so the Navajo. *Diné* faded back into their canyonlands. Along the perimeters of New Spain the Navajos again turned their lives around. They obtained domestic livestock from Spanish herds. Then, giving less time to farming, they followed flocks of sheep across their vast tablelands. They melded their values with a marvelous, huge animal that was cheaply kept, easily trained and proudly ridden as fast as the wind.

Navajos afoot were formidable enough, but mounted on swift horses they became, in a grudging Spanish compliment, "The lords of the earth." Neither Spain, Mexico, nor the United States during its first seventeen years of sovereignty in the Southwest succeeded in defeating or dominating the Navajo people.

Their subjugation was brought about by a military strategy now called "scorched earth." In 1863 Colonel Kit Carson swept through Navajoland killing sheep and horses, destroying field crops and homes, and felling whole orchards of peach trees. Only then, at the brink of starvation, did Navajos in substantial numbers submit. In March of 1864, approximately half the tribe — some 8,000 men, women and children — trudged The Long Walk, 350 miles to Fort Sumner, New Mexico, where officials again thought to convert them to agriculture.

The experiment failed. The soil of the concentration camp was salty. Crops withered. Livestock sickened. Comanche, Mexican and Anglo bandits preyed upon the Navajo. Over a period of four years, 2,000 *diné* died. When costs of feeding the Indians grew prohibitive, Lt. Gen. William T. Sherman (he of the march to the sea through Georgia), arrived to make treaty. Navajo leader Barboncito, ill, hungry, impoverished, eloquently pleaded for his people.

"I hope to God you will not ask me to go to any country except my own . . . I would like to go back the same road we came . . . After we get back to our country it will brighten up again and the Navajos will be as happy as the land, black clouds will rise and there will be plenty of rain, corn will grow in abundance and everything look happy."

The return of the Navajo was allowed — to burned homes, to the bones of butchered stock, to the skeletons of girdled fruit trees. For the 12,000 surviving tribespeople, it was the blackest hour in Navajo history. Their recovery in the next 60 years is largely an unsung saga. Beginning in 1869 with an issue of government sheep, the Navajos managed to restore their livestock industry

2. *A Navajo medicine man meters the colorful dry grits and powders which comprise a ritual sandpainting — some of whose forms are seen in modern tapestry weaves.*

and to increase their own population to 35,000 self-sufficient citizens by 1930.

And again hard times shadowed the Navajo nation. Multiplying herds over-grazed the land, dictating a drastic stock reduction. Overnight, prosperous Navajo families were impoverished. Not until World War II and its exagger-ated demand for manpower, did Navajo fortunes much improve. During the war, 3,600 Navajos served in armed forces, and 15,000 more labored in defense plants. Meanwhile, conditions on the reservation changed little. While postwar America boomed, the Navajo endured chronic problems: tuberculosis, land depletion, poverty, malnutrition. In 1948 there were fewer than 600 full-time jobs for 60,000 Navajos. Hospital beds numbered 460. In a reservation the size of West Virginia were exactly 95 miles of paved road. Of 20,000 school-age chil-dren, only 6,000 were enrolled.

Today, not "everything look happy," but the *Navajo Times* boasts, "Better

3

living conditions now prevail throughout the reservation. The People have schools and hospitals. Paved roads now crisscross the land. A $15 million dollar sawmill and other industries furnish employment for many Navajos. Tribal parks, civic centers and other recreational facilities provide pleasure for thousands. . . . Through valuable oil, uranium, coal, helium and other resources, including the education of their young men and women, the tribe has the means to progress to even greater heights."

Modern Navajoland, as the larger nation of which it is a part, exhibits endless contradiction. Every generality is vulnerable. Shining success accompanies mirrored frustration. The aged hermit who has never seen a train is not typical; neither are the college graduates administering a multi-million-dollar tribal budget. Longtime sympathizers with the Navajo people learn to accept them as individuals, and to acquire a personal, if fragmented, almanac of impressions.

They number nearly 135,000 today, more than ten times the population at repatriation. Far from vanishing, they are increasing by three and one-half percent annually, at thrice the national birth rate.

Once a many-voiced alliance of extended families, the Navajo nation now governs itself through a tribal chairman elected at large, and by regional representatives to a council. Discovery of petroleum in the 1920s led to the formation of the first Navajo central government.

Nearly half of the Navajo people are in school. Median age of the tribe is seventeen years.

At an electronics plant near Window Rock, Indians produce hardware which assists in placing men on the moon. Nearby dwell elders who steadfastly believe their ancestors created the sun by setting afire a huge turquoise.

"Literacy" in Navajoland requires fine definition. Only half of the people speak and write English, but ninety-seven percent are fluent in a native language so complex that Navajo radiomen in the Pacific during World War II openly transmitted military secrets and battle orders, a code that was never broken by the Japanese.

Although new homes are rising in settlements throughout the reservation, eighty percent of Navajo dwellings are without running water. The hogan, a circular, domed, single-room structure of earth-capped logs, poles or stone, is still commonplace. Fried bread, "the pancake of the poor," stretches a diet of mutton and goat, cultivated and wild vegetables, fruits and nuts and staples and sweets from the trading post. In general the Navajo diet is deemed to be deficient in calcium, iron and protein.

Into the mid-1970s nearly six Navajo families in ten were living on incomes below the poverty line designated by the federal government. The average number of rooms for a Navajo household was two. The average number of people in a Navajo household: five. The infant mortality rate: thrice the national average. Life span: substantially less than the national expectancy. Paved roads: 1,400 miles — so few that fifty boarding schools must operate. Unemployment and underemployment among able-bodied Navajos fluctuates between fifty-five and sixty-five percent.

Despite a sad past and imperfect present, Navajos tend to be hospitable toward outsiders. Official tribal policy welcomes visitors to camp and fish, and enjoy such spectacles as Canyon de Chelly and Monument Valley. A great-grandson of Barboncito drives a Navajo six-day tour bus. He guides paleface tourists to azure lakes stocked with Navajo trout but he will not eat fish, into which *diné* were transformed during the Great Flood. If skeptics ask how Navajos became human again, Barboncito's great-grandson asks for the name of Cain's wife.

Medicine men and women are lawfully recognized as healers in the states where they practice, and rightly so. The recitation of just one ceremony, "The Mountain Way," treatment for epilepsy, requires the equivalent of memorizing exactly the Episcopal Book of Common Prayer. The rite lasts nine days, with 500 songs of twelve verses each. Of about thirty such ceremonies, one healer can master no more than six or eight in a lifetime.

Every summer some 45,000 Navajos leave the reservation in search of work. Many are migrant farm laborers who hoe sugar beets and cultivate truck crops and harvest broom corn, peanuts, cucumbers and potatoes.

In acquiring such a personal almanac, inevitably a friend of the Navajo people will experience an episode similar to this:

Into the Tribal Arts and Crafts Center at Window Rock Mrs. Daisy Taugelchee brings her newest masterpiece of weaving, a three-by-five-foot rug. She receives a wholesale price of $1,600 for her work. Tourists gasp.

They do not realize that for her $1,600 Mrs. Taugelchee raised her sheep, sheared them, washed and carded the wool, spun the yarn, and spent every available minute of eighteen months in weaving a fabric that in many respects symbolizes the soul of the undaunted *diné*.

How Navajo Women Learned to Weave

SPELLBINDING STORYTELLERS, the Navajo. According to legend:

"Spider Woman instructed the Navajo women how to weave on a loom which Spider Man told them how to make. The crosspoles were made of sky and earth cords, the warp sticks of sun rays, the healds of rock crystal and sheet lightning. The batten was a sun halo, white shell made the comb. There were four spindles: one a stick of zigzag lightning with a whorl of cannel coal; one a stick of flash lightning with a whorl of turquoise; a third had a stick of sheet lightning with a whorl of abalone; a rain streamer formed the stick of the fourth, and its whorl was white shell."

Not so romantic is the opinion of the pioneering scholar of Navajo textiles, Charles Avery Amsden. In a 1935 magazine article he wrote:

"Navajo weaving began, if we really want to go down to the roots, long before the Navajo tribe was known in its present location, or had ever learned anything about loom weaving. The Pueblo people, who were the remote ancestors of those living today, first practiced this great craft in the Southwest, using cotton instead of the wool of later times.

"Where they (the Puebloans) learned to cultivate cotton, and spin and weave it, is more than we can say, but it is perfectly plain to archaeologists who find cotton blankets buried with their dead that they were at it at least a thousand years ago and have kept at it down to this day. No trace of the Navajo can be found in those early times, none in fact until almost the time of the Spanish discovery and conquest of the Southwest."

3. *Weaver demonstration at the Heard Museum in Phoenix, Arizona.*

As revealed by archaeology, prehistoric basketmakers artfully wove sandals, bags, nets and robes of refined plant fibers, furs and feathers. Weaving of artistic designs and textures flowered among Pueblo III peoples, A.D. 1050–1300. Their descendants continued to weave on unique vertical looms during the centuries that the Navajos were infiltrating puebloan territory from the north.

Apparently the first generations of Navajos in the Southwest were unschooled in spinning and weaving textiles. Modern Navajos dispute this theory, but the burden of scientific evidence suggests that those early nomads had little patience for cotton-growing or cloth-weaving.

It was Spain that introduced the catalyst — the sheep — which would alter forever the course of Southwestern weaving, and Navajo lifeways. Following a long-standing policy of making colonies self-sufficient and profitable, the Spaniards brought sheep by the thousands from Mexico, and decreed that their subjects should weave with wool. Submissive puebloans obliged.

Concurrently the Navajos, instinctive hunters and gatherers, acquired some sheep and found them good to eat. By raid and barter they added to their flocks to such an extent that by the mid-1500s *diné* were largely a pastoral people, augmenting their mutton diet by trade and casual agriculture. Whether they wove in such early times is conjectural.

Social upheaval and cultural exchange preoccupied Southwestern peoples during the late 1600s. For once, the pueblos turned on their Spanish masters and drove them back into Mexico. Similarly, Navajos joined in the rebellion. For afterward, pueblo people in fear of reprisal took refuge among their Navajo allies. Such fraternizing accelerated when the Spaniards returned with a vengeance in 1692. During these decades of coexistence and intermarriage it is assumed that Navajos learned to weave with wool.

Much mystery has been made of the transfer of weaving talent from one sex to another. Pueblo weavers were, and are, men. Navajo weavers were, and are, women. The explanation is logical enough to Martin Link, curator of today's Navajo Tribal Museum in Window Rock:

"Pueblo men were the cultivators of cotton, and it seemed proper that they should utilize the product of their labor.

"When Navajos obtained sheep the men probably considered it beneath their dignity to sit around all day and take care of a flock of tame animals. So the sheep were given to the women and children for care. Gradually the women came to own the sheep. It followed that if women owned the animals, they owned the wool. So to a great extent the women became Navajo weavers."

4. *Of Pueblo style, this all-wool, handspun blanket was collected by W. C. Powell during the 1871–72 exploration of the Colorado River. Natural white, indigo blue, natural black, 70 x 51 inches, several patches.* COURTESY SAN DIEGO MUSEUM OF MAN

5. First phase chief blanket, circa 1840–1850, all native handspun, brown, white and blue uninterrupted stripes, border-to-border, 48½ x 82 inches. COURTESY THE SOUTHWEST MUSEUM

Whether Navajos were weaving prior to 1700, the craft was well enough along to deserve mention in a 1706 report of the governor of New Mexico. Sketchy references to Navajo weaving are found in Spanish documents through the 1700s. By 1795 Governor Fernando de Chacon wrote of the Navajo, "They have increased their horse herds considerably, they sow much and on good fields; they work their wool with more delicacy and taste than the Spaniards." Production of Navajo fabrics soared, and trade of blankets and garments dominated Navajo economy. By 1812 a Spanish writer in New Mexico admitted, "Navajo woolen fabrics are the most valuable in our province, and Sonora and Chihuahua as well."

While gaining in popularity abroad, Navajo weaving remained essentially non-European. The spinning was done by hand on a shaft-and-whorl spindle. The foundation yarn (warp) was strung on an upright loom manipulated by simple wooden rods. The woven yarn (weft) was tamped down with a flat

6. *In a conservative example of a second phase chief blanket, circa 1870–1880,* bayeta *bars intrude border-to-border indigo and natural white bands, 46 x 56 inches.* COURTESY MUSEUM OF NORTHERN ARIZONA

7. *In full glory is this third phase chief blanket with terraced diamond and symmetrical angles intruding stripes, circa 1860–1870, of handspun natural white and brown, indigo-dyed handspun, and three-ply rose commercial Saxony yarn, 51 x 69 inches.* COURTESY SAN DIEGO MUSEUM OF MAN

batten board. Fabric edges were dressed with extra, twisted yarns. In later times two important Spanish importations were metal shears for fleecing, and metal carders for combing the wool prior to spinning.

Alas, for many a Navajo, their mastery of weaving resulted in enslavement. Through the mid-1800s goodly numbers of Navajo women were captured and impressed into service in the private homes and fabric factories of newly-independent Mexico.

Says Martin Link of those dark days, "The slaves were made to weave what their captors dictated, and out of this period emerged a type called the 'slave blanket,' decidedly Mexican in style. Although examples are rare today, their production must have been enormous, because government records speak of 'bales upon bales' of such fabrics being carted off to Chihuahua and points south."

Most authorities today regard fragments from Massacre Cave, Canyon del Muerto, northeastern Arizona, to be the most accurately dated pieces of old Navajo weaving. The relic of an 1804–5 slaughter of Navajos by Spanish soldiers, the remnant (see figure 8) bears traits of technique and design thought to be of Navajo origin.

Displayed at the Museum of Northern Arizona in Flagstaff, is a fragment of a patchwork shoulder blanket, found by Leland C. Wyman in Canyon de Chelly in 1933. Upon an original blanket of brown wool with white stripes were sewn a grab-bag of fabrics — one scrap as coarse as burlap, a corner of a Hopi woman's dress, and possibly a swatch of fine, imported Spanish cloth. On the basis of design and dyes, curators believe some of the fragments may predate Massacre Cave.

"Despite the fact that there are as yet no earlier examples of Navajo textiles," writes Clara Lee Tanner, "the Massacre Cave pieces indicate a tradition of long standing in materials and decoration. . . . The concensus is that plain tapestry weave, natural wool colors, a little native dye, indigo, and bayeta, and simple striped patterns predominated until the middle of the nineteenth century."

In the following century, as exemplified by their weaving, the genius of the Navajo people for adaptation would be supremely tempted and tested.

8. *Among the earliest dated Navajo weaves is this dress fragment recovered from Canyon del Muerto's Massacre Cave where Spaniards had slain a number of Indians in 1804–05. The Museum of Northern Arizona has a patchwork cloak, found in Canyon de Chelly by Leland C. Wyman in 1933 which may, on the basis of design and dyes, contain fragments of weaving that predate this Massacre Cave remnant.* COURTESY MUSEUM OF NORTHERN ARIZONA

From Dingy Sheep to Exquisite Rug

JUST AS THE NAVAJO people defeat generality, so does their weaving. For every rule regarding Navajo rugs there are rule-breakers. That said, construction of Navajo fabric has remained remarkably constant. For some 275 years there have occurred no marked changes in weaving, especially in the preliminary stages.

Excellent, definitive studies of Navajo weaving are in print. One, *Working With the Wool* by Noël Bennett and Tiana Bighorse, explains precisely, step by step, how a Navajo rug can be woven — even by non-Indians. Other books analyze techniques of individual weavers, past and present.

But for this introduction, risking exceptions, generally a Navajo rug passes through these phases from fleece to floor:

GROWING THE WOOL

Less so than in the past, stockraising continues as an important Navajo industry. The imported Spanish peasant breed that comprised original Navajo flocks were scrawny of flesh but long and straight of wool. Such fleeces tended to tangle and attract debris in the arid, thorny Southwestern pastures; but once clean, *churro* wool was ideal for spinning. During the late 1800s the American government issued strains of Spanish Merino and French Rambouillet. The common Navajo type of this day yields better mutton but shorter, kinkier wool, not the easiest raw material for weaving. These sheep produce shorter fibers but about twice as much wool by weight. As of old, the herding is left to women and girls, who by custom, come into ownership of individual sheep.

9. *Sheep graze the grounds of Window Rock, the Navajo capital.*

Usually in May or June the sheep are sheared when the fleece is thickest. In early times the wool was cut with a knife or sharpened metal scrap; now it is done with simple shears resembling lawn clippers. Snipping from neck to tail the shearer tries to keep the fleece intact. Best wool for weaving is from the back, shoulders and flanks. Fiber deemed too short for hand-spinning is sold by the bag to traders and to tribal cooperatives for resale as far away as Japan.

CLEANING

Vigorous shaking is sometimes all that's required to remove grit and twigs. Burrs must be removed by hand. A native soap, of yucca root extract, chases dirt without driving out the lanolin, which gives a Navajo rug its long life. The wool is fluffed and dried in a hot sun, said to make it stretch better in spinning. To whiten wool some weavers sprinkle it with kaolin or gypsum.

CARDING

Cards made commercially are thin boards armed with myriad wire teeth and fastened with handles. A wad of tangled wool is placed on one card, then repeatedly combed between the two until fibers lay in the same direction. At this step natural gray wool is obtained by carding light and dark wool together. The wool comes off the cards in a fluffy roll. Hand carding adds to the uniformity and strength of Navajo yarns. Carding further cleans the wool, but it's the weaver's hardest chore, so today many weavers buy precarded wool from the traders.

SPINNING

The spinning wheel is unknown to the Navajo. In its place is a relic inherited from those days when Navajos traveled light. The spindle is a stick about twenty inches long. Near one end of the stick is a wooden disc which acts as a flywheel when the right hand rubs the spindle against the right thigh. Meantime the left hand feeds carded wool onto the long, pointed end of the spindle. All the while the spinner adjusts the tension on the strand to achieve uniform size. Navajo homespun, with a left-hand twist, is opposite most other Indian homespun and commerial yarns, which are right-handed.

All Navajo yarn is spun at least twice; some three and four times (up to ten times for tapestries), with each spinning improving tightness, smoothness and fineness. Foundation yarn, called warp, must be respun several times.

10. *Before an octagonal hogan which once served as a guest house for Hubbell Trading Post, Elizabeth Kirk combs white wool with metal-toothed carders.*

11. *A ballet of the hands accompanies the spinning of carded wool upon a wooden spindle. Inertia is imparted to the flywheel by working the spindle against the thigh.*

DYEING

The Navajo passion for color has been satisfied in complicated ways down through the years. Red flannel by the wagonload was raveled and retwisted in early times, and as discussed in Chapter 4, garish fads invaded Navajo weaving when commercially dyed yarns reached the trading posts. Today weavers may restrict themselves to natural white, brown and black, or mixtures of these. They may use aniline dyes from the white man's world. Or, as the trend seems to be, they may draw upon a hundred or more natural dye recipes which utilize the roots, bark, flowers, leaves and fruit of plants of their region. Vegetal dyeing might be repeated daily for as long as a week. Dyes are set with various chemicals, sometimes in earlier days an acid such as urine.

SETTING UP THE LOOM

As depicted in detail in the accompanying sketch, the Navajo vertical loom consists of a sturdy frame within which are suspended, joined and anchored, a series of horizontal wooden bars, each with a vital function. A pair of conveniently spaced trees might serve as frame posts. For winter work the loom might be anchored by stones buried beneath the earthen hogan floor. Sets of foundation warps are arranged between upper and lower loom bars. One advantage of the vertical loom is constant control over the tension applied to the warps.

Alternating warps are separated by a shed rod. This separation can be reversed by pulling on the heddle, attached by loose loops to alternating sets of warps.

As in most arts, the foundation is crucial to success. In a fine contemporary Navajo rug three by five feet, the warps may total 240. This requires 400 yards of handspun yarn — four lengths of a football field. All this, and weaving is yet to begin.

WEAVING

By pushing the shed rod, or pulling on the heddle, alternating sets of warp are moved back and forth. A batten, a swordlike stick of polished and shaped hardwood, further separates these sets of warps, to allow insertion of the horizontal weft threads. Weaving begins at the bottom, the weaver drawing upon a mental image of the complete rug. Weft threads are pounded down with a wooden comb and a batten. As the warps are moved back and forth they disappear under the wefts, giving the Navajo weave its distinctive tapestry finish. By custom the weaver sits on soft skins of goat or sheep. She weaves off small

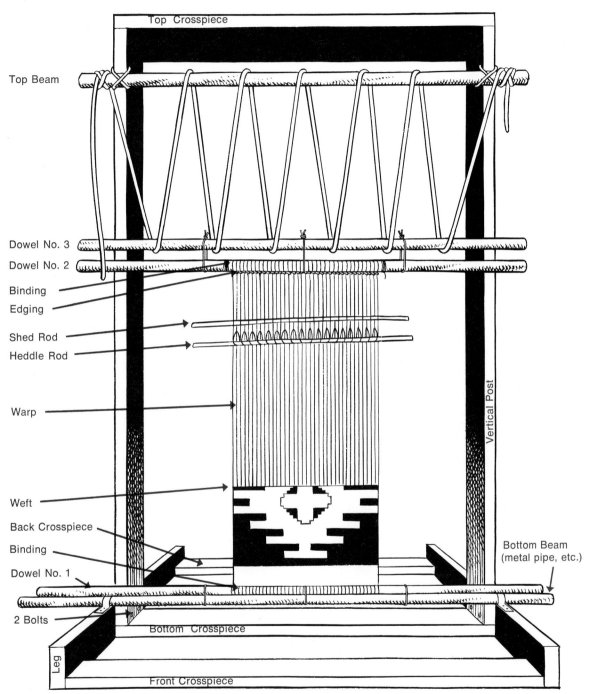

Top Crosspiece

Top Beam

Dowel No. 3

Dowel No. 2

Binding

Edging

Shed Rod

Heddle Rod

Warp

Vertical Post

Weft

Back Crosspiece

Binding

Dowel No. 1

2 Bolts

Bottom Beam
(metal pipe, etc.)

Bottom Crosspiece

Leg

Front Crosspiece

12. *Reprinted from* Working With the Wool. *Northland Press, 1971.*

19

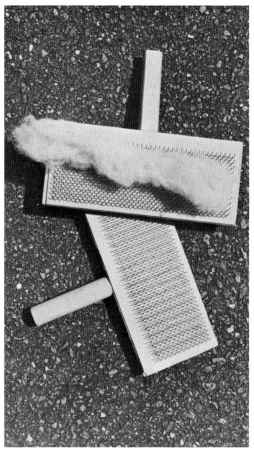

13. *These shears, 13½ inches overall, made in Sheffield, England, are commonly sold in Navajo country.*

14. *Two cards of a type still widely used by Navajo weavers are these 9½-inch-wide products of E. B. Frye & Son of Wilton, New Hampshire. This set sold for $7.50.*

balls of weft of natural color or dyed. When the work rises higher than she can reach, she may slacken the tension bar and sew fast the completed section to the lower loom bar or the loom bars may be adjusted to lower the work level. Again the warp is tightened and the weaving continues. But now her design reference is hidden; she must remember where she went, to know where to go. The last few inches of weft are inserted from the top down. For this, a needle may be used. Along most Navajo weaves are edges reinforced with extra, twisted warps, characteristically of the same yarn that forms the main background design color.

15. *Traditionally whittled by menfolk of weavers, hardwood combs come in sizes to fit every hand and weaving need. Tines must match the spacing of warp threads on loom.*

16. *Spindle is 33 inches long, of commercial doweling and homemade flywheel. The larger batten won a blue ribbon at the Museum of Northern Arizona Navajo Craftsman Show.*

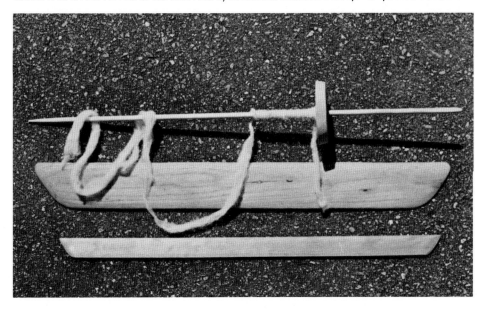

Weaver at Hubbell Trading Post works on a re-creation of an original 19th century rug.

Aside from regular tapestry weaving on a standard loom arrangement some Navajo women specialize in other techniques of long-standing tradition. Several variations of twill weaving go into saddle blankets and larger rugs. An array of as many as five heddles lets the weaver choose unequal sets of warps, such as, under-three, over-one, to produce textured diamonds, terraces and zig-zags. In such rugs designs of the two faces of the fabric are the same, but the colors are opposed.

Mental concentration plus manual dexterity go into the so-called "two-face" rug. Again, with multiple heddles, a few weavers today produce rugs of different colors *and* designs on the two faces. Gaining in acceptance, among artists and admirers, is the "raised-outline" weave, in which color and design are enhanced by an etched effect of raised wefts.

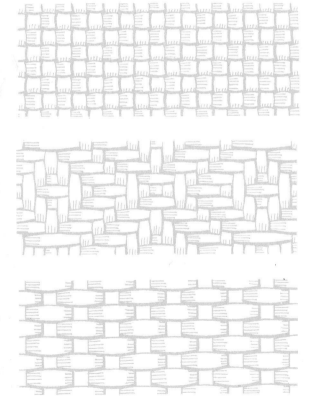

18. *Among the eight distinct Navajo weaves is the plain or* basket *weave, commonplace and probably the oldest. Warp and weft are equally distinct in the finished fabric.*

19. *Also quite common is the diamond twill, borrowed from Puebloan weavers. A relief pattern is created by arranging the heddles to elevate groups of warp.*

20. *Another familiar pattern is the tapestry weave. The warp is covered by beating down the weft to compress the threads together. It is a plain but very effective weave.*

23

Pueblo Looms,
Spanish Sheep, Navajo Artistry

"IT OFTEN HAPPENS," observes Martin Link, "that when a culture experiences strife, stress and chaos, the people turn to their art to express themselves eloquently. Some of the best of literature, painting and architecture was produced by societies enduring hard times. This is the history of Navajo weaving. While Navajo religion, economy, life-style and land base were under attack, weaving art reached new peaks of achievement."

The Classic Period, experts call it. Although arbitrarily bracketed between the years 1850 and 1870, some authorities believe the tradition of excellence was established as early as 1800. Material examples are scarce, but it is supposed that Navajos were splendid spinners and weavers of tapestry fabrics modestly beautified by border-to-border natural colors.

Indigo dye from Europe arrived in the Southwest in the early 1800s, and some of the rich, deep blue began appearing as end stripes on Navajo blankets. By mid-century vegetal yellows and greens were occasionally used along with natural white, brown and black wool. Many Classic Period weaves were of single strand, handspun wool. Black wool might be darkened with a mixture of sumac, ochre and piñon pitch. Extract of goldenrod mixed with indigo made green. A sunny yellow was derived from rabbit brush blossoms.

But nothing brightened up Navajo weaving so much as *bayeta* red.

A myth persists that early Navajo weavers removed red uniforms from the

21. *Classic serape, circa 1870, tightly woven to the texture of canvas, containing natural white handspun, indigo handspun, yellow, green and red Saxony and 5½-inch bands of red* bayeta *near each end, 48½ x 68 inches.* COURTESY GIL MULL

22. *Classic child's shawl of great diversity of handspun in natural colors, both plain and carded together. Indigo-dyed handspun together with several types and colors of commercial yarns, 30 x 55 inches.* COURTESY GIL MULL

bodies of slain Spanish soldiers, and converted the wool into blankets. In truth, all the armies of Spain couldn't have supplied enough red uniforms for the Classic Period. And no self-respecting Navajo would touch an item tainted by *ch'įįdii,* the ghost of death.

The story of *bayeta* is romantic enough, and undoubtedly far-fetched. In limited amounts it may have reached Navajoland in the form of red flannel underwear, which the Indians had no qualms against pilfering from Spanish clotheslines. Perhaps some weavers unraveled some longjohns and threaded the strands into new blanket patterns. At any rate, the Spaniards, detecting a demand, began importing English-made baize, via Spain and Mexico. It arrived by the bolt, as *bayeta,* a scarlet-to-crimson answer to every red-loving Navajo's prayer. *Bayeta's* color was imparted by the dye, cochineal, extracted from dry, crushed insects native to Mexico and other warm climates.

Incredibly, Navajo weavers so treasured *bayeta,* they would ravel the cloth strand by strand. Then they would twist together two, three and sometimes four or more thin plies of *bayeta* to form multi-ply weft yarn. Even so, the bulk of Classic Period fabric was built upon single-ply, fine homespun.

26

Turkish flannels, English serges and Mexican yarns, although inferior, competed with *bayeta*. In fact, much of what is considered *bayeta* today may be of American trade goods. As American presence grew, wagons groaning with bolts of sleazy Eastern woolens traveled 800 miles down the Santa Fe trail toward a tribe of weavers who literally could make something out of nothing.

The ingenuity of Classic weaving is demonstrated in a child's shawl, thirty by fifty-five inches, now in the collection of Charles G. Mull. The warp consists of five distinctly different types of yarn: brown handspun, soft maroon and white Saxony, a tightly twisted yellow three-ply yarn, and a very tightly twisted white three-ply yarn. Some warps were paired; others as single strands.

No less than eleven different wool materials form the weft, handspun,

23. *Classic serape in rare poncho style is modeled by Mabel O'Dell, noted weaving restorer of McIntosh, New Mexico. The blanket, circa 1840–50, contains cochineal-dyed bayeta of two shades, indigo-dyed handspun and white natural handspun, 55 x 83 inches.* COURTESY GILL MULL

24. *A serape of 1890 period is designed with a combination of serrated styles of early weaving, but the cotton warp diamond lozenges and vertical arrangement suggest a later date, all handspun of natural white and aniline black, red and orange, 51 x 70 inches.* COURTESY GIL MULL

raveled and commercial. Speculates Mull, "The extreme diversity of yarns in this blanket suggests that the weaver was scraping the bottom of the barrel for every bit of available material. The almost total absence of white handspun wool, even in the warp, suggests a scarcity. It is tempting to wonder if this blanket could have been woven during the time of the Navajo captivity at Bosque Redondo (1864–68). During this period the Navajo were largely cut off from their normal supplies of wool, and machine spun Saxony yarns are reported to have been supplied from the Fort Sumner post supplies . . ."

At any rate, toward the latter part of the Classic Period the Navajos acquired their first commercial yarns. Perhaps at Fort Sumner, deprived of their flocks, weavers began to use Saxony from Germany. Almost pastel of hue and silky soft, three-ply Saxony often was combined with *bayeta* and natural handspun. Saxony also came in colors other than red.

25. *Softly uniform in weave, this serape, circa 1880–90, presents a riot of natural and aniline-dyed handspun, raveled red flannels, and green commercial yarn, 53 x 80 inches.*

COURTESY GIL MULL

Stripes remained popular throughout the Classic Period, but gradually a Mexican-like, stair-stepped diamond intruded Navajo taste. Geometric designs, beginning small, were dropped into the edge-to-edge stripes. The diamonds, zigzags enlarged until the background stripes were all but lost. This progression is most clearly followed in the so-called "chief" blanket.

Navajos had no chiefs. The blanket of that name largely was an export item, prized by Plains Indians. First cousin to the Pueblo *manta* the chief blanket was for throwing about the shoulders in foul weather. Thus worn, the stripes complimented the physique of the puniest brave. To more easily form these stripes, Navajo weavers made the warp dimension the shortest so that wefts could be run from edge to edge. Black, white, indigo blue and *bayeta* culminated in a final phase of "chief" boasting elaborate crosses, triangles and diamonds. An estimated ninety percent of "chief" and other wearing blankets were traded to

26. *A woman's dress consists of two rectangles of handwoven black wool bearing identical end-patterns of aniline-dyed red, stitched together but with openings at the top and upper corners for head and arms.* COURTESY SAN DIEGO MUSEUM OF MAN

Cheyenne, Kiowa, Sioux, Comanche and Arapaho Indians rich enough to afford them, and to other men who wanted to appear larger than life.

Less striking garments were also woven, some for Navajo use. Muted designs marked women's wear, usually three bands of repeated designs, running the width of the blanket. Another traditional clothing for women of this time was the *biil,* a dress made of two identical, rectangular blankets. Custom decreed that a broad black center band would be bracketed by bands of red, preferably *bayeta.* The idea for the *biil* may have survived a time when Navajo women wore two animal furs sewn together as a poncho with holes for head and arms.

The most astonishing product of the Classic Period was the *bayeta* serape, a radical departure in design and color from the calm natural stripes of Pueblo origin. Exactly when and how the idea of terraced diamond motifs arrived in the Southwest is conjectural. The first examples of the Navajo *bayeta* serape are tentatively dated from 1830–1850.

"The *bayeta* serape was an object produced to astound and impress," writes Mary Hunt Kahlenberg and Anthony Berlant. "Fine, rare materials influenced the elaborateness of design and inspired weaving of the highest quality. Patterns in the *bayeta* serape literally burst across the blanket. . . . The design often appears as a variation of superimposed diamonds over stripes." Frequently the background is of raveled *bayeta* woven into horizontal stripes of blue and white.

Of similar serape shape was another exceptional blanket, the Classic Period "moki." Hinting of Pueblo genius, the pattern was of black, brown and blue weft stripes. Parallelograms of white and red in later years were inserted to break up the stripes, but relative to the *bayeta* serape, the "moki," from an old term for the Hopi Pueblo Indians, remained a conservative product of the Classic Period.

The decline and near collapse of Navajo weaving during the last third of the nineteenth century is ascribed to many factors. At repatriation from Fort Sumner, Navajo flocks numbered fewer than two thousand head. Trading posts came to the reservation in the 1870s and the railroad in the 1880s. Commercial yarns, dyed in a rainbow of colors and ready to weave, tempted weavers into shortcuts and wild experiments. By 1890 weavers had come under tremendous economic pressure to cater to the preconceptions — however preposterous — that white tourists held of Indian design. One result: if an Indian craft, surely it must be covered with swastikas, arrows and superstitious signs. Through the Transition Period of some of the worst of Navajo weaving, it would take the women about twenty years to recapture their art from tasteless patrons.

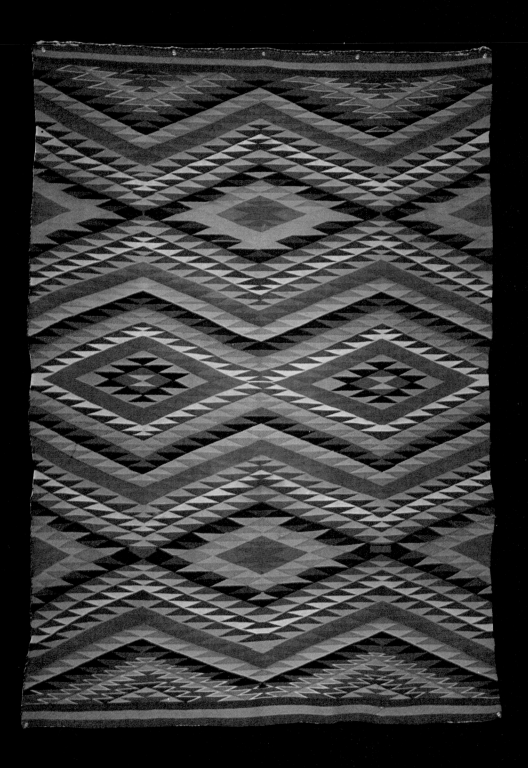

The Blanket That Went on the Floor

RAW, IRRESISTABLE CHANGE was thrust upon the Navajo nation in the years of Fort Sumner and afterward. Majority histories refer to the process as the civilizing of the wild West.

But in countless ways for Indian people the intrusion of an industrialized society was disastrous, demeaning and demoralizing. "Improvements," well-intended as they may have been by Americans and their government, in some ways altered Indian life for the better, but as often as not something of value was lost. For the Navajo, one price of Americanization was classic weaving.

Until about 1875 the products of Navajo looms were blankets for their own wear and for trading to other Indians. By the 1880s stores operated by white traders sprang up in the most remote corners of the reservation. The shelves of the trading posts offered clothing, utensils and processed food. Inexpensive, machine-made blankets from Pendleton, Oregon, appealed to women who heretofore might spend half a year weaving a blanket of similar size. The art of weaving might have perished altogether had it not been for another factor in the trading business — the demand by tourists for Indian curios. Trainloads of white customers were sold native crafts by the ton by large firms such as the Fred Harvey Company. Far away from the railroad a Navajo weaver might wear a cotton skirt, velvet blouse and Pendleton blanket, but her handwork would bring cash and credit at her trading post. Some enterprising traders stimulated sales with the mailing of brochures with pictures of available weaves.

27. *The essence of Germantown is this serape entirely of commercial wool yarn in ten colors on a cotton warp, circa 1899–1900, 52/54 x 74 inches.* COURTESY GIL MULL

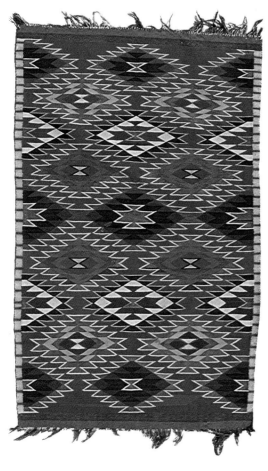

28. *An eye-dazzler whose rich Germantown commercial wool colors are enhanced by outlining of the Teec Nos Pos style, bears serrated, overall diamond patterns and fringes sewn on after weaving, 34½ x 155 inches.* COURTESY SAN DIEGO MUSEUM OF MAN

From the beginning of this commerce traders influenced what buyers wanted. In time, what buyers wanted, buyers got. They demanded pillow faces, lap robes and bed covers. Some blankets of high quality continued to be made, but the rush was toward inferior, quickly woven items for decorating white homes.

And if homespun was scarce, or required so much time and work, the trader had another answer: commercial yarns — dyed, spun, twisted and ready to weave. Called "Germantown" after the textile center in Pennsylvania, the full spectrum of aniline-dyed, three- and four-ply yarns was imported. Navajo weavers went on a color binge. It was as if artists limited all their lives to black, red, blue and white suddenly held palettes daubed with fifty hues. In explosive "eye-dazzlers" and other intense, expressionistic styles, Navajo weavers out did one another in creating optical effects.

29. *This fancy table runner is a fringed textile of Germantown yarns in a design dominated by a multi-hued, eight-pointed star, circa 1890, 25 x 39 inches.* COURTESY SAN DIEGO MUSEUM OF MAN

Germantown yarn was expensive: aniline dye was cheap. Sold for the first time in bulk in the 1880s, aniline dyes derived from coal tar were simple to use (just toss the packet into boiling water, sometimes envelope and all), garish, and exactly what white folks wanted in authentic Navajo rugs — lots of bright color. For the first time in substantial amounts Navajo weavers substituted commercial cotton twine for the stronger wool warp spun by hand.

Designs also gave way to new ideas. Instead of the right-angle terraces of the Classic Period, Navajo weaving came to be dominated by the smooth-sided diamond and triangle. This *serrate* or diamond pattern often ran the length of the weave.

Nudged by the businessman in the middle, by 1890 both weavers and customers came to consider a Navajo tapestry a suitable covering for a floor. This transformation of blanket to rug affected size, texture and design. For one

35

30. *A* yeibichai *rug made in 1942 between Oraibi and Indian Wells, Arizona, is of handspun wool warp, and wefts of handspun in natural white, black and brown, and more handspun in aniline colors, 78 x 142 inches.* COURTESY SAN DIEGO MUSEUM OF MAN

thing, rugs seemed more proper with borders.

In a gross departure from their long tradition of abstract design, Navajo weavers obliged public demand with a new kind of rug: the pictorial. They wove American flags, trading post signs, mottos, figures of cows, horses, houses, birds, bows and arrows and cowboys. In 1896 with the completion of the Denver and Rio Grande Railroad into Durango, the high point of the celebration was the presentation of a Navajo blanket depicting a five-car passenger train and a railroad station in each corner. Strongly opposed by fellow tribesmen, weavers just after the turn of the century began to picture *Yeis,* Navajo divinities, in their rugs.

The mid-1880s brought a reduction in the use of commercial yarns. Navajo flocks had multiplied and local wool was abundant. The reservation in general produced weaves of everdeclining quality. A common practice of traders was to purchase rugs by weight, with little regard for the success of design or technique. For these "pound blankets" wholesalers paid from twenty-five cents to two dollars and fifty cents per pound. As human as any other people, the Navajos soon learned that a rug greasy with lanolin and laden with sand would bring more than a clean fabric of careful construction.

31. *Evidence of a troubled time is this "pound" blanket of heavy hand-spun on cotton warp, circa 1880, filled with the cultural conflicts of border-to-border stripes, frets, swastikas and lozenges, 61 x 64 inches.*
AUTHOR'S COLLECTION

Although much maligned in some some accounts of Navajo history, traders as best they could probably saved and eventually revitalized Navajo weaving.

Among early champions of quality work were Lorenzo Hubbell of Ganado, and J. B. Moore of Crystal. At Chinle, beginning about 1920, through the efforts of white helpers and Indian experimenters, interest was rekindled in vegetal dyes. Formulas by the score were perfected using ingredients of nature. Although few of the concoctions likely were used in early times, the muted colors are somewhat remindful of some found in antique Southwestern weaving.

In the half century between 1920 and 1970 the clearest direction for Navajo rugs was identification of types by geographic origin. Again, the trader played a role. After World War II rug designs and types became standardized around trading posts such as Two Gray Hills, Wide Ruin, and Teec Nos Pos. By no means were all rugs tied to a reservation region, but the trend was strong, fueled by maturing appreciation of collectors and neighborhood pride of weavers.

As always, economic forces continued to influence Navajo weaving. During the Great Depression a relative few weavers remained at their looms despite miserable rewards. Yet it was during these years that the largest Navajo rug in history was constructed, by the Joe family of Greasewood. In a special stone

32. *Well-made wedgeweave blanket of the 1880s is entirely of handspun, natural brown and white, and dyed with indigo, aniline red and possibly, vegetal yellow. Also called pulled-warp construction, the weave is characterized by scalloped edges, 61 x 62 inches.*

COURTESY GIL MULL

house forty feet long Julia Joe and her two daughters, Lilly and Emma, began processing the wool. Beginning in 1932 the women sheared sixty white sheep and eighteen black. Two full years went into carding, spinning and dyeing. Then, from sunrise to midnight for three years and three weeks the women wove their masterpiece, a seamless rug measuring twenty-six by thirty-six feet and weighing two hundred fifty pounds.

For their heroic labor they earned about ten cents an hour. In 1938 a trader kept an accounting of a typical weaver's investment of time, and he concluded that she was making no more than a dollar a day.

According to veteran trader Russell Foutz, Navajo textile art fell into hard times again in the 1950s, when long-staple wool had become scarce. Foutz attributes a revival to the breeding of native ewes to Lincoln rams, noted for longer, kinkier wool. And:

"It was only after commercial yarn was made available that many women who had never made a rug before started to weave. A great number of them learned their art by weaving with Germantown, and then graduated to handspun as they became more expert.

"I am convinced that if it had not been for commercially prepared wool

33. *A late classic serape in typical* moki *pattern, is of natural white and brown-black handspun, indigo handspun and raveled American flannel, circa 1875, 52 x 72 inches.*
COURTESY GIL MULL

34. *An eye-dazzler rug in a rainbow of hand-spun in natural, indigo and hues of aniline, plus a center stripe of dark rose* bayeta, *with commercial tassels, in serrated diamond patterns and pre-1890 Greek fret borders, 45 x 71 inches.* COURTESY GIL MULL

35. As a page from Gil Mull's original 1911 J. B. Moore rug catalog attests, Navajo weavings sold by the square foot in the early years of this century. Shown on the opposite page is a matching rug which has left Mull's ownership to take a place in the Denver Museum of Natural History.

there is no doubt that Navajo weaving would be a lost art today."

In flux as always, Navajo weaving today seems to be breaking out of a system which presumed that women of certain areas would weave specific patterns. Contemporary weavers are well-traveled and some dwell far from place of birth. Provincial loyalties are being replaced by a new sense of Navajo *nation*. The women attend fairs and exhibitions where their weaves are shown side-by-side. Just as a New England dory can be manufactured in San Diego, so may a Teec Nos Pos outline pattern grace a loom at Kayenta.

The happy reality of these times is that Navajo women in goodly numbers have elevated their inheritance once again to an art form. As in the past, the weavers have adapted borrowed ideas and new designs and varied techniques within their ever-dynamic craft. For once the doomsayers were wrong. In the 1970s the best Navajo weaving compares with the finest of the Classic Period.

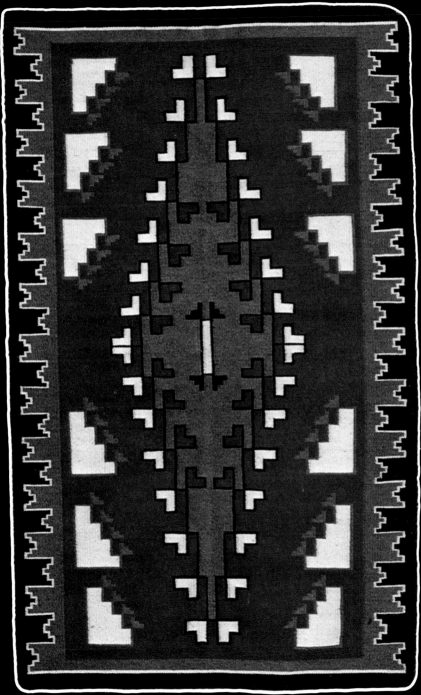

𝓒ontemporary is 𝓒osmopolitan

ON A TOUR of his old haunts, a long time white trader recently stopped at a trading post near Shiprock, New Mexico. He was surprised to note that not one sandpainting rug — for which the region is famed — was in view.

"Where are all your ceremonial rugs?" the extrader asked the current trader.

"Don't have any," was the reply. "All my weavers are making Two Gray Hills. That's what the public wants!"

For many years two tiny settlements in the far western end of Navajoland were the source of a special kind of weave called "raised outline" in which color design is emphasized by a thickening of weft. Now weavers at Ganado, halfway across the reservation, produce raised outline rugs and the fretted, bordered pattern associated with Ganado may come from anywhere. When that self-same old trader wanted a Tuba City storm pattern rug for his own collection, he commissioned it to be done from a photograph by a weaver at Old Sawmill.

Although geographic names no longer guarantee origin, the terms are still appropriate and useful. Weavers, exhibitors, traders and buyers continue to categorize by regional name if not by region. Of course some weaves, notably saddle blankets, never were limited to a locale. Today as in the past these items may originate almost any place.

Given the gamut of commercial yarns and dyes, contemporary weavers have endless variety of color. Much of the raw material is home-grown; the

36. The elongated central diamond of a typical red Ganado is captured in a modern weaving by Elizabeth and Helen Kirk, of handspun native wool, and predyed commercial "wool-top" also handspun, 36 x 60 inches. COURTESY HUBBELL TRADING POST

sheep population of the Navajo nation is stabilized at about two million head.

As throughout the past, nearly all current production is of simple tapestry weave; that is, weft passes over and under alternating warps throughout entire rugs. The weft threads are tamped down with a wooden comb and batten, so as to hide the warp. The most popular shape is rectangular, with warps running the longer dimension.

Prices are rising for better weaves year by year, and many artisans are turning out smaller pieces, away from gigantic rugs, toward a size and weight of the Classic Period shoulder blanket. Another modern trend is the creation from beginning to end of weavings obviously intended for hanging. The blanket that went on the floor now goes on the wall.

As for regional types, the blurring of production areas probably will result in the disappearance of some, and an increase in others, depending upon what is in demand. Five years ago the storm pattern was in vogue. Less so today. As Navajos have known since they arrived in the Southwest, change is the unchanging element in their culture.

In 1963 Indian trader Gilbert Maxwell coined a term, "the general rug." His rough estimate was that rug production was fifty percent saddle blankets; twenty-five percent general rugs; twenty-five percent specific and distinctive as to type and region. "The general rug," he wrote, "is the rug whose design, quality and color do not distinguish it as being from any particular locale. They may be plain stripes or geometric patterns with or without a border. Such rugs are made throughout the reservation."

A decade later, in the opinion of museum curator Martin Link, the production percentages have become ten percent saddle blankets, fifty percent general rugs, and forty percent rugs recognizable as regional types. So-called "natural" rugs of black and white and mixed gray handspun may originate from nearly every reservation region.

REGIONAL RUGS

GANADO

If contemporary weaving boasts a capital, it is Ganado, just south of the geographical center of the Navajo nation. No better introduction to the evolution and status of Navajo textiles exists on the reservation than Hubbell Trading Post just west of Ganado. It is also an ideal place for learning about Navajo ways.

Now a National Historic Site under park service supervision, Hubbell's is the oldest continuously operating trading post on the reservation. It was estab-

37. *Dating to the 1870s the famous trading post of J. Lorenzo Hubbell at Ganado is today under the protection of the National Park Service; the post continues to serve the needs of Navajos.*

lished in 1876, and existing buildings date to turn-of-century. Indians travel from miles around to shop among the tobacco tins, "can goods," horsecollars, kerosene lanterns and bolts of velvet. To Hubbell's they still bring their wool, their rugs, their jewelry, their crops of piñon nuts. For the Navajo people the Hubbell post is a social center, gossip exchange and political forum. The Navajo tongue freely commingles with tourist talk. In the stone-and-sod adjoining warehouse women handspin yarn and weave on upright looms. Rugs representative of all sections of the reservation are stacked shoulder-high in the rug room where for nearly a century woven Navajo masterworks have been bought and sold.

Fashionable as it is to malign the white trader among Indians, Don Lorenzo Hubbell's role among the Navajo community was friend, champion, helper. Of a family of New Mexican traders, Hubbell dared to take over a store in a hostile land beyond the protection of the U.S. Army in 1876. He survived and prospered because he was fair, wise, ambitious and more than a little lucky. Once he was tied to a post for death by torture and was saved only by the unlikely arrival of a Navajo friend.

Don Lorenzo was more than a trader. He brought the best of literature and art to his remote and humble home. To his table were attracted President Theodore Roosevelt, painters, sculptors, writers, scientists and philosophers. Hubbell was active in Arizona politics. When the papers of statehood were signed in Washington in 1912, directly behind President Taft stood Don Lorenzo.

A crossroads of commerce met at his rambling hacienda. He freighted goods 200 miles. He issued his own aluminum money. Indian herders and craftsmen depended upon Hubbell's just heart and fluent Navajo. During bleak economic slumps, Hubbell cheered weavers by insisting upon and paying for quality work. Through the 1880s Hubbell regularly resold $25,000 worth of rugs a year to the Fred Harvey Company. At times the blanket room was piled to the ceiling.

"Collecting is a disease," Don Lorenzo's daughter once said. "In this case, the whole family caught it."

The trading post became an archive of the best of arts and crafts, and today it is virtually as Hubbell left it, hung with rare Southwestern blankets, stocked with guns, furnished with antiques of surprising elegance, enriched by a library of scarce Americana and decorated by originals of famous Western painters.

The experience of a visitor to Hubbell's is of participation, thanks to an arrangement by which the nonprofit Southwestern Parks and Monuments Asso-

38. *This is a one-of-a-kind rug usually done in Ganado red, but on impulse produced in blue by Mary Begay and Grace Henderson Nez in 1974, 48 x 72 inches, 1974 price of $985.* COURTESY HUBBELL TRADING POST

39. *An old motif in a brand-new weave is this third phase chief blanket of hand-spun, predyed, processed wool by Elizabeth Kirk and Helen Davis, 48 x 48 inches.* COURTESY HUBBELL TRADING POST

ciation operates the trading post as an old-fashioned business. At this writing the post is run by Bill Young, more than fifty years a trader among the Navajo. He is assisted by his son, John.

"We're most pleased with one project which doesn't cost taxpayers a dime," says Bill Young. "Our goal is the replacement of all the floor rugs in the Hubbell home with exact copies. The originals can be saved from the damage of foot traffic, but visitors can still admire the home as it was when Don Lorenzo lived in it."

Working for hourly wages, two Navajo weavers — sometimes more — work in the trading post warehouse. They spin warp of Navajo wool, and weft from commercial skeins. Then, with the original rugs as models they weave duplicates, color by color, design by design. They faithfully repeat the individual flairs and flaws of the original weavers. Thus far seven large rugs have been donated to retire original Hubbell rugs to museum care.

Don Lorenzo liked red. Generally he encouraged the weavers within his purview to limit themselves to natural colors: white, gray and black. But the tradition of *bayeta* was established, so Hubbell made one concession to aniline dye, so long as it was red, a hue so strikingly rich, dark and bold, it came to be called "Ganado Red." To heighten the dramatic impact of large areas of red, Ganado weavers would also run their black wool through aniline black.

The serrate, or stair-stepped diamond came to dominate Ganado style. In some pieces one diamond is drawn out from one end to the other; in others three adjoining or interlocking diamonds fill most of the space. Don Lorenzo considered a rug design properly contained within borders, so the Ganado type often had a plain border of black or red, plus an inner border bearing a clean geometric repetition. Crosses, frets, triangles, zig-zags, streaks and chevrons are typical within areas unfilled by diamonds.

Once Ganado was noted for its large rugs, and some big ones are still done — a Hubbell entry for the 1974 arts and crafts show of the Museum of Northern Arizona measured ten by fifteen feet. According to Maxwell, a large Ganado, twenty-four by thirty-six feet, was made in four years by four weavers in the 1920s. The trend at present is toward smaller, simplified weaves, some suitable for wall display. Quite a bit of white goes into Ganado weaving generally, although some old pieces were sensational with just Ganado red and dyed black.

The rug of the Kayenta area once was considered a regional type by authorities such as Gilbert Maxwell. First cousin to the Ganado, it had a white background with one large diamond or several smaller ones, in natural gray, intensi-

40. *This Klagetoh by Grace Henderson Nez, 48 x 70½ inches, had a 1974 price of $3,000.* COURTESY MUSEUM SHOP, MUSEUM OF NORTHERN ARIZONA

fied black and aniline red, lacking the richness of Ganado red. Borders often were doubled and undecorated. The central motif typically was serrated. When at the turn of the century Kayenta women were still struggling with borders, they tossed in a few extra end bands for good measure. This was carried over in some Kayenta weaving into recent times.

Today Bill Young can count at least one hundred superior weavers active in the 1970s in the Ganado sphere. In recent times Louise Begay, Grace Henderson Nez, Mary Begay, Faye Yazzie, Mary Amma Jones, Elsie Wilson and Sadie Curtis have woven on the Hubbell looms. Other prize-winning Ganado style weavers were Stella Toadachini, Maggie Begay, Marie Begay, and Esther Whipple. Annia Yazzie, Clara Jim and Nellie Roan were well known for their old-style Klagetoh designs quite similar to Ganado types inspired by Don Lorenzo.

Size alone came to distinguish the rugs of a group of weavers at Piñon to the north of Keams Canyon, very near the center of Navajoland. Kate Peck Kent tells of an example fifteen by thirty feet in size, and Maxwell measured another that was fourteen by twenty-six. Borders, colors and designs are pure Ganado: natural white, gray and black; the black intensifies a red produced from aniline dyes. Few large weaves have been made in recent years, and the Keams Canyon classification is becoming obsolete.

Positioned between two areas where vegetal dyes are commercially successful, the weavers of Ganado are also turning out borderless tapestries in earthy colors drawn from nature. The weavers of Klagetoh, once famous for Ganado-region rugs, have come under the influence of the vegetal dye revival at Wide Ruin. The Ganado region of weaving extends to the east and southwest to include the communities of Cornfields, Sunrise Springs, Navajo Station, Lower Greasewood and White Cone.

CRYSTAL

Within the wooded flanks of the Chuska Mountains, due north of the Navajo capital of Window Rock, perches Crystal, another trading post important to Navajo weaving. Crystal is remote, but like all other trading posts, it is more accessible today than in the past. From 1897 to 1911 J. B. Moore, the Crystal trader, educated scores of Navajo women in the weaving of rugs in styles which Eastern housewives presumed Indian patterns to be.

One tale has Moore obtaining a shipment of square-foot linoleum samples bearing patterns from Persian rugs. Moore issued the patterns, along with strong hints that he wouldn't buy anything else. Soon Moore's rug room was

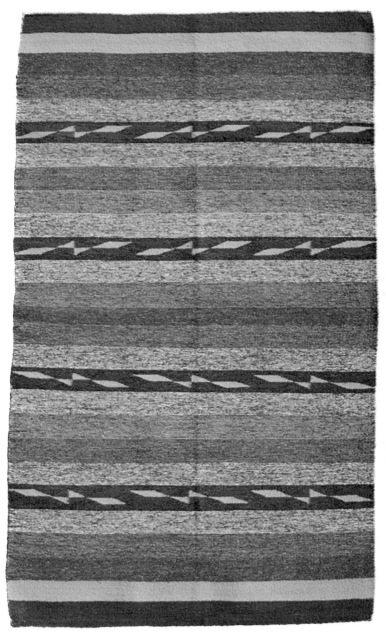

41. *A modern Crystal by Mary Moore has border-to-border designs in muted hues of vegetal dyes, 37 x 63 inches, 1974 price of $550.*
COURTESY MUSEUM SHOP, MUSEUM OF NORTHERN ARIZONA

stacked with weaves done in a "genuine" Navajo design that would have fit on the floor of Omar Khayyam's tent. Strong borders, plain or fancy, were customary around mostly light-colored grounds. A strong central diamond extended into busy, doodlelike line designs, most characteristically terminating in angular hooks resembling the letter G. Like Hubbell, Moore had no objection to red. He even shipped wool for refinement off the reservation, then supervised the dyeing at Crystal. Nearly all oldstyle Crystals contain red as well as white, gray and brown-black.

Moore is thought to be the first to distribute a mail-order catalog of color illustrations of Navajo rugs. The finest Crystal weave in 1911, of about twenty-two square feet and weighing seven pounds, was sold for twenty dollars. Today a rare old Crystal in linoleum square pattern might be appraised at six hundred to one thousand dollars.

After Moore gave up his trading post his tradition continued in the Crystal region. Renewed interest in weaving in the late 1930s and 1940s involved vegetal dyes. Again there is a Crystal-type regional rug, but it is radically different from the old Moore style. In the newer pieces there are no borders. Designs are edge-to-edge bands of earthy colors which seem extracted from a painted desert landscape. In a single weaving there may be rusty red, chocolate, natural gray, milky green, and a pastel vegetal pink. Within some bands are simple, geometric, repeated designs such as flat triangles or rhomboids. In some, bands may be wavy lines effected by alternating two or three wefts of contrasting colors.

Of all contemporary Navajo weaves, the Crystal type fits most quietly into modern home decorating. Some present-day Crystal rugs are nearly square, but most are rectangular. The yarn is handspun, giving a nubby feel to the finished fabric. Two fine modern Crystal weavers are Mary Arthur and Faye C. George.

TWO GRAY HILLS

Navajos have a way with names. One of their peaks is called Roof-Shaped Mountain on the Run. A sluggish stream is named Water Without Ambition. A place where wagons tended to bog down in sand is known as Where the Mexican Wept. On the east side of the reservation the two gray hills identifying the most refined and expensive textile of Navajoland are near a trading post of the same name, south of Beautiful Mountain and east of Flows into the Rocks Lake. In the Two Gray Hills region, including Toadlena and Tocito, sandstone and lava are sculpted into canyons and spires, and mountains rise to bear alpine conifers.

42. *An intermediate type of Two Gray Hills, circa 1945, in dyed black, natural white, and two shades of brown and grey by carding natural wools together, 46 x 63½ inches.* COURTESY SAN DIEGO MUSEUM OF MAN

It was to this spectacular and isolated province that the patterns of J. B. Moore migrated eastward from Crystal, to evolve into one of the best known and most prized Navajo textiles. Maxwell credits two competing traders, George Bloomfield and Ed Davies, with providing the inspiration and instruction with which the weavers transformed their nondescript early rugs into the premium Navajo fabric by the mid-1920s. If so, these traders would have gotten nowhere without willing weavers who "kept their hands in the wool." Perhaps it is not accidental that quality weaving continued among Navajos far removed from the cultural shocks visited upon residents closer to roads and rails.

The Two Gray Hills of this day is a technical and artistic masterpiece. Native wool in natural colors is intensively carded and spun as fine as thread. Weft counts of 120–150 per inch have been noted, as fine as cashmere and linen. By comparison, superior weaving elsewhere on the reservation may contain no more than 30–50 wefts per inch. Refinement of the Two Gray Hills type has been inversely proportionate to size. Rugs five feet by seven were about standard in the 1930s. Only well-to-do collectors can afford a weaving of that size today. Thus, many Two Gray Hills rugs are made small, and are properly considered tapestries.

Colors are white, black, brown, tan and gray. Subtle variations of shading are achieved by carding black with white, and brown with white. Within one rug as many as a half dozen tans may be manipulated. In a few rare examples other colors have appeared, but because they did not sell well those colors were eliminated.

By now, design has become so complex as to defy a general description. Traditionally the outer border is black, intensified by dye, in a plain band. Inside this border is a second border of light ground, broken up with repeated geometric symbols: frets, squares, terraced chevrons, zig-zags. A third and fourth border band may mirror these themes in negative and positive treatment of color.

A favored motif of the enclosed rectangle is an elongated diamond, busily divided and extended by stair-stepped loops and hooks. Triangles and squares which fill out the rug corners sometimes refer to some aspect of the central diamond. Judges look for precise symmetry; when folded end to end or lengthwise the halved patterns of better Two Gray Hills weaves will match nearly perfectly. Yet no two rugs are ever exactly alike.

This individual handling of each weaving within a regional convention is little appreciated off the reservation, yet it occurs today, and always has. With a

43. *There are no two identical rugs woven in the Two Gray Hills style — here is a unique work by premier weaver Daisy Taugelchee.*
COURTESY
READ MULLAN COLLECTION

44. *A Two Gray Hills tapestry of first rank is this 1974 creation by Dorothy Mike, one of the better modern weavers, with threads spun as many as ten times to equal fineness of linen, 25 x 37 inches, 1974 price of $3,000.* COURTESY MUSEUM SHOP, MUSEUM OF NORTHERN ARIZONA

little study a white man can learn to recognize "Navajo rugs." Gaining more knowledge he might identify "A Navajo rug, of the Two Gray Hills type." But the fuller response is to perceive the uniqueness of weave within each controlled creation. It is art.

In art museums Da Vincis and Rembrandts and Picassos are not thrown on the floor to be trampled by viewers. The works of masters are safely displayed and carefully lighted at eye level. Since the bulk of Navajo weaving was purchased for utility as well as beauty, mainstream America tends to regard it as a quaint craft–industry, rather than a form of art. Within too many institutions of natural history and anthropology artistic Navajo weavings are stored out of sight, emerging only for study as objects of culture or economy. One exception: under glass in the Denver Art Museum, a permanent place of honor is given a Two Gray Hills rug by Daisy Taugelchee, artist.

At present there may be as many as a hundred excellent weavers of Two

Gray Hills tapestries, and here some of the best are listed. Among them are Julia Jumbo, Julia Theadore, Mary Tom, Daisy Taugelchee, Priscilla Taugelchee, Mary Gilmore, Mildred Natoni, Mary Joe and Mary Louise Gould, and Elizabeth Mute.

CHINLE

Due north of Ganado on State Highway 63 Chinle sprawls at the mouth of Canyon de Chelly, a holy place to Navajos. A national monument but still under Navajo ownership, Canyon de Chelly was the last retreat of *diné* during their times of greatest trouble. The canyon slashes a series of gorges into the red sandstone of the Defiance Plateu. Sheer, smooth walls rise nearly a thousand feet to surround monolithic spires taller than New York skyscrapers. Ancient ruins cling to niches in the mineral-stained walls.

On the valley floor and beyond the mouth of the canyon Navajos dwell in old-style hogans and newer, square houses with turquoise colored roofs. They raise vegetables and fruit, and tend herds of sheep whose best wool is saved for the rugs of the Chinle region. Chinle weaving extends from Many Farms on the north to Nazlini on the south.

In the memory of oldtimers Chinle rugs were tightly packed and of generally good quality from the turn of the century to the 1930s. As for design, they were undistinguishable from rugs made throughout the reservation: black border, big central diamond in terraced red, gray and black.

"I was in Chinle when the change took place," recalls Tom Kirk, of a large and highly regarded family of Indian traders. "Cozy McSparron and others at the Thunderbird Ranch encouraged the weavers to try soft, pastel colors, and weave in borderless designs with bands reaching from edge to edge. For a while Cozy had a bunch of weavers making rugs his way, while across the hill, Garcia's trading post had them weaving the usual black-gray-red. In time, Cozy's idea won out."

Acceptance of the muted colors did not come easily. McSparron experimented with vegetal dyes, and Mary Cabot Wheelright inveigled the Du Pont company into producing dyes in pastel shades for Navajo use. The Du Pont dyes proved to be unsatisfactory for use by unschooled weavers, but one of McSparron's concepts—edge-to-edge banding—dramatically changed Chinle weaving.

Credited with giving Navajo women an array of practical vegetal dyes is Mrs. Nonabah G. Bryan. While teaching weaving at Wingate school, Mrs. Bryan, a Navajo, tested numerous recipes for vegetal dyes during the 1930s.

45. *Doubly distinguished is this two-faced weave in Wide Ruin style, in border-to-border stripes and small geometric designs, by Mabel Burnside Myers.*

COURTESY READ MULLAN COLLECTION

Classes at Wingate in the middle of that decade were instructed in their preparation and application. In 1940 Mrs. Bryan published a booklet detailing the formulas for eighty-four shades derived from organic and mineral materials native to Navajoland. The work has been advanced by others, notably Mabel Myers, a Navajo, and today the formulas number in the hundreds. Tree bark, flower petals, bulb skins, pine needles, leaves, lichen, corn kernels, berries, cactus fruit, walnut shells — each source contributes its own hue from nature. Mordants to set the dyes are urine, raw alum, and juniper ashes.

At Chinle today most weavers spin and dye their yarn. The weft is relatively coarse and during weaving weft threads are not packed down hard. The result is a thick, textured rug. Some weavers incorporate the Crystal wavy-line weft treatment into band designs. Along with the earthy browns, yellows and reds, and subtle greens and grays, Chinle weavers use some brighter aniline colors, and a tasteful amount of white. Typically, in the same rug, groups of plain stripes will separate bands adorned with repeated, terraced diamonds.

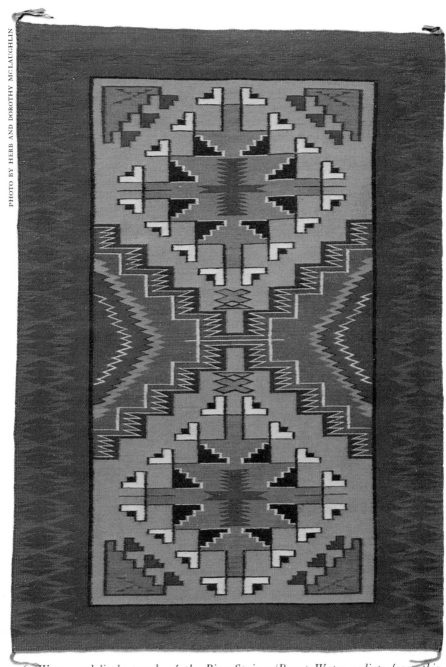

46. *Warm and lively trends of the Pine Springs/Burnt Water radiate from this tapestry in vegetal dyes by Philomena Yazzie, winner of first prizes at the 1971 New Mexico State Fair and 1972 Arizona State Fair.* COURTESY READ MULLAN COLLECTION

Another region participating in the so-called vegetal revival surrounds the trading posts of Wide Ruin, Burnt Water and Pine Springs. This land of cedar breaks, sandy water courses and rolling roadways lies along the south-central border of Navajoland.

When, in 1938, Bill and Sallie Wagner Lippincott took over the Wide Ruin post, they induced their weavers to turn to colors extracted from nature and imparted to reservation-grown wool. The Lippincotts refused to accept inferior weaving. They encouraged a return to old-style design elements — connected diamonds and triangles, lines of rhomboids, and alternating straight lines extending from edge to edge without a border. Although some bordered tapestries nowadays are elaborations of patterns introduced by Hubbell at Ganado, the hundred excellent weavers of this region manufacture mostly borderless rugs.

The restrained ochre, sepia and umber hues combined with muted blues and grays gives weaves of this region a character of quiet elegance. Ellen Smith, Lottie Thompson, Nellie Roan, Marjorie Spencer, Blanche Hale, Philomena Yazzie, and Maggie Price are among the better weavers of this region.

47. Two-faced Wide Ruin rug by Agnes Smith of natural and vegetal-dyed handspun yarn, with 35 wefts per inch each side, 23 x 39 inches. COURTESY RAY GWILLIAM COLLECTION

PHOTO BY HERB AND DOROTHY MCLAUGHLIN

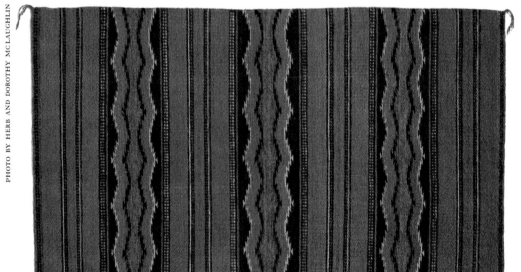

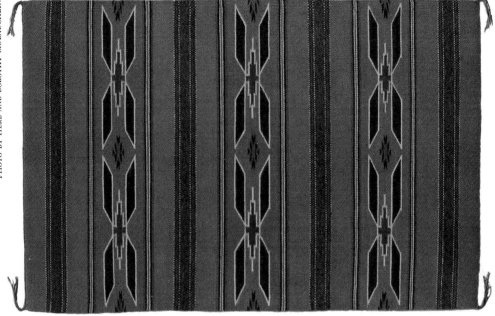

48. *A vegetal-dyed handspun by Ellen Smith.* COURTESY RAY GWILLIAM COLLECTION

49. *A touch of pink excites this Wide Ruin type done in 1960 by Lottie Thompson.* *Stripes of tiny trapezoids are reminiscent of Navajo weaving of more than a century ago.* COURTESY READ MULLAN COLLECTION

50. *A black and gold border brightens this weaving by Hilda Begay in Teec Nos Pos style, 27 wefts per inch, 55 x 72 inches.* COURTESY RAY GWILLIAM COLLECTION

TEEC NOS POS

Northernmost of the Navajo weaving regions is Teec Nos Pos (Circle of Cottonwoods) near Four Corners, where Arizona, Utah, Colorado and New Mexico join at a common point. (At this National Monument it is possible for an agile visitor to occupy, on hands and knees, four states at once.) Only in recent years have paved roads penetrated the sweeping valleys and broken mesas of the San Juan River country. The weaving region encompasses the area around Teec Nos Pos, Arizona, and Beclabito, New Mexico. With energy-hungry municipalities drawing upon the rich reserves of oil, gas and coal of Four Corners, the past decade has brought wrenching change to Teec Nos Pos.

Yet prevailing there is a kind of rug dating to the 1890s. The origin is lost, but that was a time when traders were aggressively converting weavers of blankets to weavers of rugs. As with J. B. Moore at Crystal, perhaps an early trader

51. *Busy and brilliant in outlined designs is this 1970 Teec Nos Pos tapestry by Esther Williams.* COURTESY READ MULLAN COLLECTION

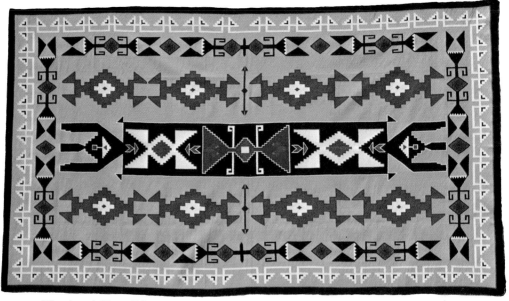

52. *Worthy of blue ribbons is this Teec Nos Pos tapestry of commercial yarns by Ruth Yabany, 85 x 144 inches.* COURTESY CLAY LOCKETT COLLECTION

passed around pictures of the kinds of rugs then most fashionable in the homes of Easterners. Undeniably, a lot of Persia appears in a Teec Nos Pos rug.

The border is wide and lavishly decorated with repeated geometrics. Some central themes fall midway between old Crystal and new Two Gray Hills patterns. Other centers are flambouyant interlocking diamonds. Amid hooked and forked zig-zag lines Teec Nos Pos weavers will scatter stylized feathers and arrows.

As if all that weren't enough, the weaves are done in bold aniline-dyed hand-spun or commercial yarns. The trademark of a Teec Nos Pos weave is the outlining of each design element with a contrasting color. Somehow, as entities unto themselves, these weaves can be quite appealing, but they blend with difficulty into home decoration.

Authorities disagree as to whether the women of Red Mesa, Sweetwater and Mexican Water to the west of Teec Nos Pos comprise a separate region of weaving. In the past their designs and colors have been less gaudy and commercial. But as in Teec Nos Pos pieces, Red Mesa rugs boast extra wide borders, centers with diamonds, and outlined designs.

The region of weaving on the west side of Navajoland is as large as some Eastern states. Roughly the region is 120 by 50 miles, from Coppermine on the west to Chilchinbito on the east, from Kaibito on the north to Tuba City on the south. Other weaving centers in this region are Shonto, Inscription House, Kerley's Trading Post, Cameron, The Gap, Paiute Mesa, Navajo Mountain and Cedar Ridge. For these far-flung communities Tuba City functions as something of a secondary capital.

Exciting innovation has bypassed the weaving of the west. Prevailing styles are early 1900s — conventional geometric with borders in black, white, brown and gray in natural tones, and aniline red. Vegetal dyes occasionally are employed, but there seems to be no acceleration in this direction. No better saddle blanket is made than that of Inscription House.

The best-known, easiest-recognized pattern of the west is the Tuba City Storm, which is woven at other places as well as around Tuba City. No style has

53. *Ella Yazzie Bia of White Clay, Arizona, was commissioned to copy a design in Read Mullan's catalog. In six months the job was done but with tiny differences in design, 39 x 63 inches.* COURTESY TOM E. KIRK COLLECTION

54. *Genesis of storm pattern elements are shown in this early example, circa 1910, 46 x 60 inches.* COURTESY MUSEUM OF NORTHERN ARIZONA

attracted more contradictory lore. One tale ascribes the origin to a pattern printed on sacks of flour shipped to western Navajoland in the early days. Then again, since J. B. Moore of Crystal, New Mexico, included a storm pattern in his 1911 catalog, it may have sprung from one of his patterns. Still another possibility was a Tonalea trader with a keen appreciation for what paleface rug buyers expected in the way of Indian symbolism.

Borders of storm patterns seem electrified by zig-zags or contrasting steps. Against a usually gray background in the middle is an elaborated square ("the center of the world"). In the four corners are smaller colored squares or rectangles ("the houses of the wind, the four sacred mountains"). Strong zig-zag lines ("lightning") join the corner boxes with the center as if charging the entire rug with white, slashing thunderbolts. For extra measure some storms include swastikas and stylized water beetles.

COAL MINE MESA

Possibly the most significant novelty in Navajo weaving in the past decade gained first acceptance in the Coal Mine Mesa region southeast of Tuba City.

55. *Seemingly in action is this vi-brant raised-outline, Mary Begay weave of double-saddle proportions, 30 x 60 inches.* COURTESY

READ MULLAN COLLECTION

The technique is called raised-outline, in which additional weft thread emphasizes the outlines of designs. The region has long been known for its skilled weavers of twilled saddle blankets and two-faced rugs which display unusual treatments of weft threads.

Gilbert Maxwell credits the furtherance of raised-outline weaving to the late Dr. Ned Hatathli, Navajo educator who served as the second president of Navajo Community College.

GALLUP

Size also defines the primary weaving of the Gallup, New Mexico, region, which reaches northeastward to Tohachi, Coyote Canyon and Standing Rock in the northwestern corner of that state. Long and narrow it has always been nicknamed a "throw," and in inferior samples it deserves the additional word, "away."

Many throws are coarsely woven on commercial cotton warps of bright commercial yarns in simple designs. Lacking a strong wool foundation these throws are not serviceable as saddle blankets or covers, or as rugs. They make chair backs and table cloths. And they are relatively inexpensive.

Better throws, in the standard one and one-half by three foot size, can be starkly handsome in black, white, gray and red in balanced geometric patterns, or in abstract pictorials, such as corn stalks and ceremonial figures.

SHIPROCK

A volcanic neck rises 1,400 feet above a surrounding plain in the northeastern corner of the Navajo reservation. An imaginative paleface dubbed it Shiprock. The Navajo people have another name: Winged Rock, on which the gods swept ancestral Navajos into the sky, out of reach of enemies.

In such a land of long shadows and mystical vibrations one would expect spirits to invade Navajo weaving. In the Shiprock region, they do, although again the medicine man was a white trader. It's said that just after the turn of the century Will Evans of the Shiprock Trading Company induced weavers of the region to portray *yeis*, the supernatural beings who communicate between Navajos and their gods. From Shiprock town on the San Juan River the weaving region extends southwestward toward Rattlesnake and Red Rock.

The Shiprock *yei* customarily has a white or light-colored ground. From three to six *yei* figures — tall and slender and bearing ceremonial appurtenances

56. *This is one example of the Gallup throw rug. Homespun in natural white and aniline-dyed wool on cotton warp, the design is in red bordered with black, 19½ x 37 inches.*

57. *A two-faced* yei *rug by Martha Tsosie is entirely of handspun yarn, 20 wefts per inch, 46 x 57 inches.* COURTESY RAY GWILLIAM COLLECTION

—face outward in stiff, upright postures. There may be a border; likely not. In more elaborate *yei* rugs three sides are marked off by the elongated body of a "rainbow goddess." The first *yeis* were woven in the face of tribal opposition, inasmuch as the figures are taken directly from sandpaintings crucial to sacred ceremonials. But since no religious significance was attached to the rugs themselves, opposition evaporated, and today there seems to be no objection to the manufacture of *yeis*. They are not used in Navajo worship; they are not prayer rugs.

Large *yeis* have been made, but the trend definitely is toward a size more suitable for hanging, about three by five feet. Much smaller *yeis* have been produced in recent years.

In a carryover from the turn-of-century Germantown color binge, Shiprock *yeis* are in bright, bold hues. Commercial yarns and aniline dyes are much in evidence, and within a single weaving a dozen or more colors are used.

Markedly different from a *yei* rug is another weave taken from ceremonials,

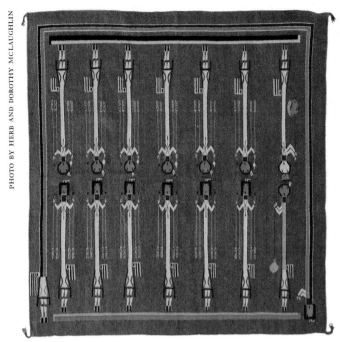

58. *A copy of the sandpainting representing the first
dancers in the Nightway Chant is by Mrs. Dan Manuelito.*
COURTESY READ MULLAN COLLECTION

called *yeibichai*. A *yei* is a deity, and a *yei* rug depicts the spirits themselves.
Navajo dancers in certain rites personify these spirits in the *yeibichai* dance.
Thus, the rug which pictures dancers is the *yeibichai* type. The figures are more
humanlike, and the action of the dance commonly is suggested by uplifted feet.
In the 1970s small *yeibichai* tapestries are done in handspun, vegetal-dyed yarns
for an attractive, understated style. A wave of the future may be this combina-
tion of natural colors with recognizable Navajo symbolism. *Yei*-weaving today
occurs far from its origin. Ribbon winners in this category at the 1974 Navajo
Show in Flagstaff were Helen Tsinnie, Tuba City and Leona Holiday, Rough
Rock.

LUKACHUKAI

Another region of *yei* weaves is the region west of the Lukachukai mountains
around the trading post of that name, and including Upper Greasewood and
Round Rock.

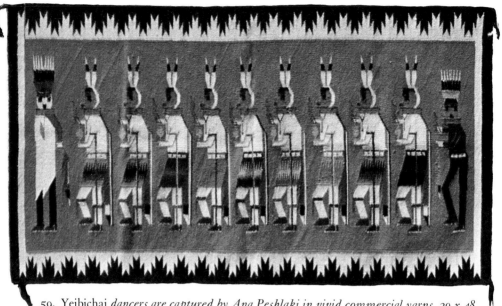

59. Yeibichai *dancers are captured by Ana Peshlaki in vivid commercial yarns, 29 x 48 inches, 1974 price of $575.* COURTESY MUSEUM SHOP, MUSEUM OF NORTHERN ARIZONA

Unlike Shiprock *yeis* the rugs of Lukachukai tend to backgrounds of dark gray, black, tan, brown or even red. Multi-colored *yei* figures are arranged in single or double rows. There may or may not be a border. Long noted as a region of handspun yarns, Lukachukai exports a true rug, thicker, nubbier and coarser than the Shiprock counterpart. White, black, brown, green, blue, yellow and red brighten the *yei* figures, and all but the white likely are aniline base. As with Shiprock weaves, sizes of Lukachukai rugs are becoming smaller. Rugs. with lifesize *yei* figures are rare.

NON-REGIONAL RUGS

TWILL WEAVING

In many areas of Navajoland weavers produce twilled textiles. Numerous loom heddles are employed to manipulate the vertical warp cords to allow weft threads to pass over and under unlike numbers of warps. Herringbones, diamonds, zig-zags and other geometric effects are achieved. The typical twill piece

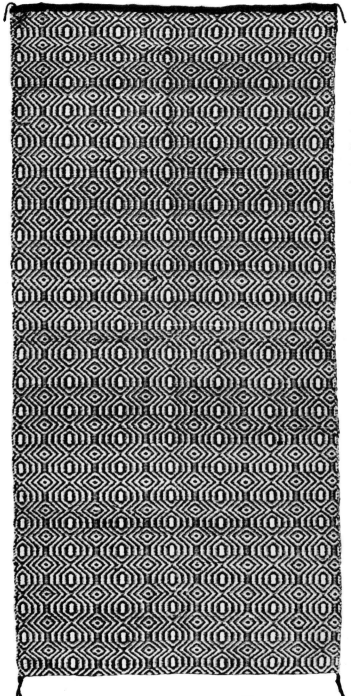

60. *Guaranteed to wear like iron is this double-saddle size twill in natural colors by Patsy Long of Canyon Diablo, Arizona, 30 x 60 inches, 1974 price of $195.* COURTESY MUSEUM SHOP, MUSEUM OF NORTHERN ARIZONA

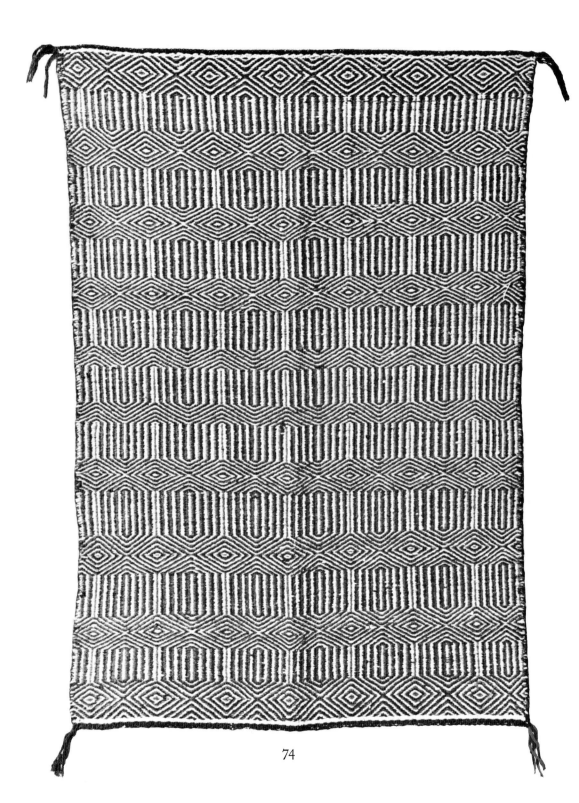

74

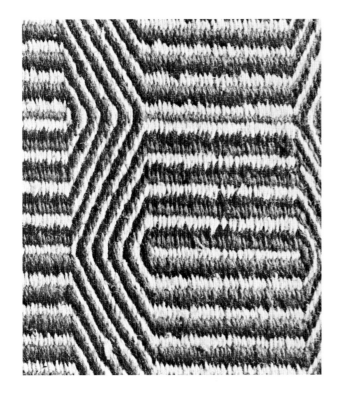

61. *A thick twill weave in red and black by Mary Anne Yazzie* (opposite page). *Close-up photo reveals complexity of stitches, 35 x 48 inches, 1974 price of $147.* COURTESY MUSEUM SHOP, MUSEUM OF NORTHERN ARIZONA

is limited to natural wool colors, although some use is made of red. Twill weaving is sometimes called double weaving as one side mirrors the other in texture and pattern.

SADDLE BLANKETS

Native weavers once provided their families with ponchos, leggings, sashes, saddle girths, saddle covers, wearing blankets, door covers and saddle blankets. Some sashes are still seen . . . Navajo women wear them under their silver concha belts to protect their velveteen blouses. But currently the only item manufactured for Navajo use is the saddle blanket.

The size is standard. A single saddle blanket is roughly thirty inches square. The double saddle is about thirty by sixty. Quality of weaving can vary greatly. Many are coarsely woven and poorly shaped. Yet in top-grade saddle blankets some of the best of contemporary weaving is represented.

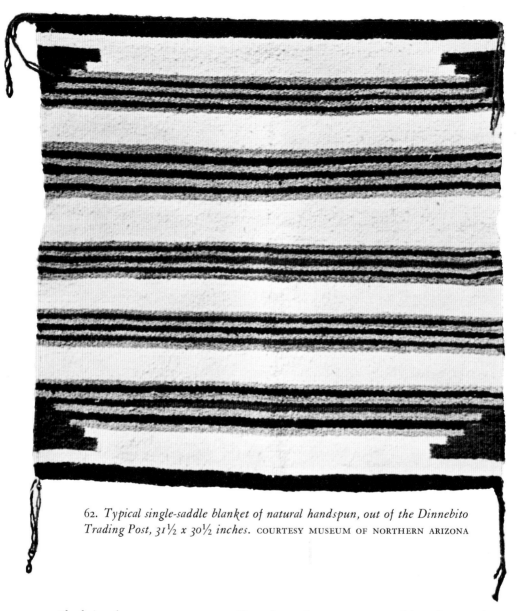

62. *Typical single-saddle blanket of natural handspun, out of the Dinnebito Trading Post, 31½ x 30½ inches.* COURTESY MUSEUM OF NORTHERN ARIZONA

If of simple tapestry weave, aniline dye colors are arranged in edge-to-edge stripes. To serve Navajo vanity colorful geometric flourishes are given saddle blanket corners, where they show beneath a saddle skirt.

Many saddle blankets are twills. For durability in day-to-day use the double weave twill is considered the best.

63. *A common double-saddle of tapestry weave in natural colors with a touch of aniline at the corners to show behind the saddle when folded, 63½ x 31 inches.*

COURTESY
MUSEUM OF NORTHERN ARIZONA

64. *To some experts there seems to be a category of weaving called "natural" in colors as they come from the sheep. The 29½ x 46 inch tufted rug (above)* by Joan Curley *is one approach; the optical illusion measuring 32 x 52 inches* (right) *is another; and yet another is the 52 x 86 inch rug* (far right) *by Alma Williams.* COURTESY MUSEUM OF NORTHERN ARIZONA

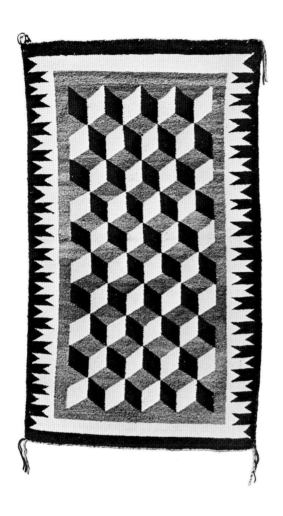

Certain weavers are willing to produce almost anything if the price is right. Recently the rug room at Hubbell's displayed a rug depicting the trading post itself in perfect three-dimensional proportion. And how did the weaver achieve perspective? Using her mind's eye as a photographic enlarger, she "blew up" a picture postcard scene of the trading post.

Through the years women have woven the American flag, mottos, landscapes, automobile emblems, optical illusions and semaphores. Occasionally a weaver will revive an old, chief pattern. There are women who still know how to produce a wedge-weave (sometimes called pulled-warp weave), with bands stacked with oblique stripes. Because this type of weaving forces the warps out of the normal vertical position, the edges of wedge-weave rugs are wavy. Wedge-weave rugs dating to the 1890s are quite rare. (See Plate 32.)

Another unusual and expensive Navajo rug weave is the two-faced. Multiple heddles are required to produce drastically different designs on the two faces of a single rug — perhaps a *yei* pattern on one face, and an allover geometric or striped pattern on the reverse. Some weavers, as in the Chinle area, are so skilled they never look at the backside of their weaving, yet their patterns come out perfectly. Audry Wilson of Ganado and Mabel Burnside Myers of Pine Springs produce excellent examples.

65. *Alma Hardy who lives near The Gap Trading Post fashioned a world of handspun wool populated and equipped with livestock, buildings, a pickup truck and a helicopter, 33 x 47½ inches, 1974 price of $750.* COURTESY MUSEUM SHOP, MUSEUM OF NORTHERN ARIZONA

66. *The weaver of this patriotic pictorial is unknown.*

COURTESY W. D. HARMSEN

PICTORIAL RUGS

In the Southwestern textile collection of the Museum of Man in San Diego is a priceless pictorial rug which exemplifies the wit, charm and practical limitations of Navajo pictorial weaving. The reproduction is a Santa Fe train. Smoke billows from the engine. A caboose brings up the rear. Birds soar above, and tracks lie below. Between are Pullman cars. Apparently some informant only partially explained how paleface people traveled cross-country in sleeping cars. The berths are correctly shown, upper and lower. But the passengers are shown sleeping standing up! (See Plate 70.)

67. *A most difficult pictorial to render, this exquisite butterfly tapestry is said to have required the labors for five years of a weaving family residing near The Gap Trading Post on the Navajo Reservation.* COURTESY THE ASHTON GALLERY

68. Ready wit of the Navajo race is expressed in this droll rank of cows by Mary Lou Billy, 23½ x 26 inches.

No matter. It looks nice. Pictorials today may be of almost anything within view: jet airplanes, meteors, flags, helicopters, domestic and wild animals, rodeo ropers. One popular theme is of a green cornstalk bearing birds, no two alike. Rugs of this kind from the Lukachukai area usually are of aniline-dyed handspun.

The tradition of picture-weaving is long-standing. In the Charles G. Mull collection a pictorial dated 1880–1890 shows two hogans, one horse and thirteen letters of the alphabet.

69. *One horse, thirteen letters of the alphabet and four hogans are among the designs placed among lightning strokes by a weaver circa 1880–90, handspun in aniline red, indigo blue and natural white, and lavender in four-ply Germantown, 41/43 x 68 inches.* COURTESY GIL MULL COLLECTION

70. *Of his famous "Railroad Blanket" in 1892 George Wharton James wrote in* Indian Blankets and Their Makers: *"That weavers* are *influenced in their choice of design by their environment I have illustrated a score or more of times, but never more forcefully than by the weaver from whom I purchased the fantastic blanket pictured in colors. . . .*

"This weaver's summer hogan *was not far from a siding on the main line of the Santa Fe Railway, some fifty miles west of Gallup, New Mexico, over the state line in Arizona.*

"One day after she had set up her loom, she was aroused from her thought by the arrival of a train going west. That immediately suggested to her that she attempt to reproduce the engine and train of cars in her blanket. The sun was glistening on the rails, and this effect she reproduced by alternations of white and blue. (Read from bottom up.) The train was of passenger coaches, and there was room on her loom for only two cars, and these of rather compressed dimensions. To denote that they were passenger cars she introduced two human figures in each. While this work was progressing certain birds appeared on the scene, together with two women, one walking east and one west. A 'light' engine also came traveling east, and as the sun happened to be shining upon it as it passed it had a bright, glistening appearance, so she represented it by weaving it in white, while the windows of the cab are picked out in dark blue. A large and small rain-cloud also appeared on the horizon and these are duly represented.

"After getting ready for the next panel and no train appearing, she pictured six flying birds alighting on the track and five walking female figures. A rain-cloud is at each end of the group of walkers. This panel is followed by one showing two engines together, going west, with flying birds and rain-clouds above them.

"The next panel shows a sleeping car. The remainder of this panel is made up of fleecy clouds, flying birds, and rain-clouds, while the last panel is her very effective representation of a poultry train going west," 27 x 47½ inches.

COURTESY SAN DIEGO MUSEUM OF MAN

The Navajo religion remains a vital part of reservation life. Ceremonial rites are kept fresh for every eventuality, ever toward enhancing the harmony of humans with the natural world. At thirteen, Navajo girls experience The Womanhood Rite signifying their arrival at puberty. Into modern times, warrior Navajos seek the Enemy Way Rite on return from battle; many a veteran of Vietnam fighting has passed through this traditional purification.

Certified healers, Navajo medicine men (and women) perform astounding feats of memory. One ceremonial consists of some 500 songs, each a twelve-verse set. To orchestrate such a ceremonial, a medicine man must memorize the equivalent of an entire Wagnerian opera — the words, the music, the lighting, the directing, the scene painting, and the stage movements of all characters, not just in a general way, but in every detail. A medicine man and apprentices may spend much of a day perfecting an intricate painting of colored sands and powders. The patient is seated on the painting, and during the healing rite, the painting is destroyed. The term sandpainting is misleading. Many ingredients besides sand are used: crushed minerals, charcoal, corn meal, pollen and pulverized blossoms. Once blessed with holy corn pollen, a sandpainting within a ceremonial hogan becomes no less than a pictorial altar ritually empowered to give or take health, or life itself.

Thus, it took great courage for the first weavers to risk incurring the wrath of the gods by defying the rule that ceremonial pictures must be destroyed. (Blindness and death were among the punishments.) Joe Ben Wheat has written that sand painting tapestries were woven for Richard Wetherill as early as 1896 at Chaco Canyon. Consensus history holds that in 1904 Hosteen Klah, a medicine man, was persuaded by Wynn Wetherill of Two Gray Hills trading post to weave a "Whirling Log" painting. Before his death in 1938 Klah is believed to have woven about twenty ceremonial designs. He also helped in preserving drawings of sandpaintings, fortunately so, for today Navajo student doctors may inspect 650 sandpainting sketches preserved at the Museum of Navajo Ceremonial Art in Santa Fe.

So strong were early taboos, one weaver of a sandpainting blanket was forced by public opinion to take her weaving sixty miles away for sale. Another story relates that in 1906 a sandpainting blanket was secretly fashioned in a bolted back room of Simpson's Trading Post on Glayo Wash. No more was the blanket done, the weaver died, reinforcing fears and discouraging this kind of

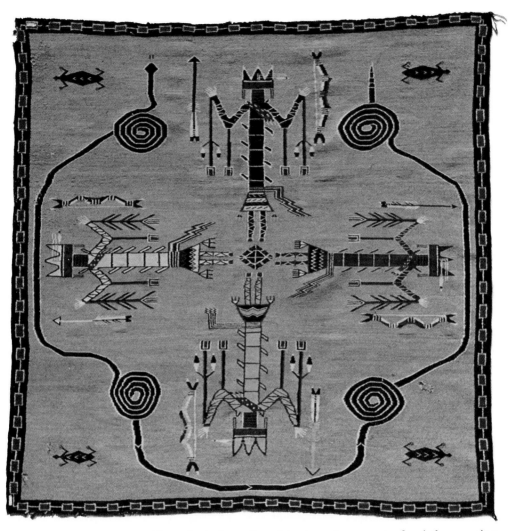

71. *The structural data on this sandpainting collected in the early 1930s speaks of the care often given in weavings of this type: all handspun, in natural white, natural wools combined as gray, black enhanced with dye, and the remaining yarns in aniline colors, 8 warps and 28 wefts per inch, 83 x 85 inches, priced 40 years ago at $350.* COURTESY SAN DIEGO MUSEUM OF MAN

weaving. The rationale today is that if such a weaving is not quite completed (or deliberately altered from the actual sandpainting), blasphemy is avoided.

Such pieces by Klah were square. His, and those of other weavers, usually are patterned upon a tan background representing neutral sand. *Yei* figures, the "rainbow goddess," sacred plants, constellations, "earth mother and sky father," and numerous animal and storm symbols go into sandpainting weaving, which in the finest quality requires extraordinary skills of the weaver. As might be suspected, these weaves command high prices. Among current award winners are Mary Song and Ruby Manuelito.

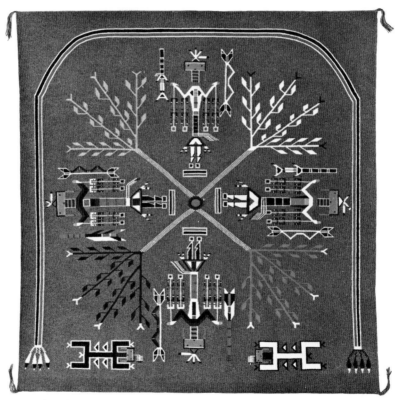

72. *A prize-winning sandpainting rug by Mary Song depicts the Whiteshell Arrow People from the Male Shooting Chant in Navajo religion. The figures bear arrows, bows and strings and stand upon short rainbows or sundogs. The roots of herbs join in the center. Over all is a rainbow garland with magpie and eagle feather terminals, 56 x 58 inches.* COURTESY DENNIS LYON

Much contradictory and confusing mythology has arisen regarding a thin line — sometimes mistaken for a flaw — which many Navajo women weave into the upper righthand corner of their rugs as they near completion. Most obvious are the lines which penetrate a border to the edge of the rug. These lines are of a contrasting color, usually of the inside background.

In basket and pottery designs such a break is of great antiquity in the Southwest. A host of explanations have been coined, some by Indians, some by whites. Traders tell believing Easterners the line is "the devil's highway," which "lets the evil spirits out." Some weavers frankly admit they add the touch because their mothers told them to, and that customers expect to find it. But otherwise it means nothing.

Fortunately, a study was pursued and published recently titled, *The Weaver's Pathway,* by Noël Bennett. Following a thorough historical search and interviews with Navajo weavers Mrs. Bennett concludes that to most women the wefted gesture allows a pathway, so that a weaver's "spirit, mind, energies and design" will not be entrapped within the completed rug. In a sense the pathway line says, "May the next weaving be even better."

73. *"The weaver's pathway," a background color leading from an inner motif to the edge of the weaving.* COURTESY MUSEUM OF NORTHERN ARIZONA

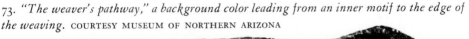

7

Whither Navajo Weaving?

THE EVERLASTING STRENGTH of the Navajo people is their genius for adaptation. While other prehistoric American peoples vanished as tribal entities, *diné* persevered. They bent to the hurricanes of change. They did not break. So they are together today, attaining self-determination, within their resource-rich refuge, stronger in numbers than ever before.

At a time when the artistic glory of long-vanished tribes reposes faded and all-but-forgotten in museums, the jewelry, painting and weaving of Navajo artisans are acclaimed from coast to coast. White writers who in their youth predicted the demise of Navajo weaving have grown gray while waiting for their dire forecasts to come true. Meantime, the weaving art prospers. An estimated 5,000 weavers finish 10,000 pieces per year. Although the sheer quantity of Navajo textiles has diminished per capita, most observers of contemporary weaving believe that the best of this day compares to the best of the classic period of a century ago. For such a resilient and renewable art, who dares to foresee its disappearance?

Not that powerful forces contrary to the weaving tradition are not at large. Electronics plants, sawmills, power generating stations, recreation enterprises and service industries are paying wages comparable to off-reservation jobs. Why weave with wool at home for twenty-five or fifty cents an hour, when wiring transistors earns ten times as much plus fringe benefits?

Weaving once was taught in schools. The courses were abolished through the 1950s and 1960s, and whereas some revivals of this training emerged in the

74. *A weaver spinning wool in the traditonal way at Hubbell's Trading Post.*

93

1970s, generally speaking the weaving art is not formally taught in schools. An exception is Navajo Community College at Tsaile, where weavers such as Mabel Burnside Myers instructs classes of sixty aspiring artisans.

Wool in bulk is in increasing demand on world markets. In a recent year Navajo shepherds sold great quantities of wool to Japan.

The close relationship between trader and weaver is being eroded. Most posts today are like town stores. Self-service. No barter. Cash and carry.

The pickup truck has replaced the horse-drawn wagon. A weaver of Chinle can go to Gallup in less than two hours. Her prize-winning rug at the annual

75. *Redoubt, homeland and spiritual sanctuary for the Navajo people is Canyon de Chelly and its tributaries, Canyon del Muerto and Monument Canyon where some still live and work in the traditional ways.*

Indian Ceremonial is analyzed by weavers who live at Dinnebito, Dinnehotsa and Tse Bonito, who also gadabout in pickup trucks. Regional ideas are freely swapped, slyly borrowed and baldly pilfered. And is this to be decried? Regional weaving types are a recent manifestation, and if they are no longer of regional origin, their regime will be quite brief.

What is traditonal? If Navajos entering the Southwest followed tradition (archaeologists insist), they would not have taken up weaving at all. If the first traditions of Navajo weavers were honored, there would be no patterns other than quiet stripes, edge to edge. Did *bayeta* finalize Navajo tradition? Or the Germantown eye-dazzler? Or handspun? Or aniline? Or vegetal? Has tradition peaked with that offspring of Persia, the Two Gray Hills? Or is a ceremonial sandpainting the final word? Or the abstract sculpted in raised outline from Coalmine Mesa?

Unquestionably, Navajo weaving will undergo further change, and one possibility is a decline. The more optimistic view is that the art is on the threshold of widespread public acceptance for what it is — an art form. The recent experience of Indian potters of the Southwest is most heartening. For centuries these potters clung to their ancestral techniques and designs while exploring fresh ways of emotional expression. They kept their art alive in a country accustomed to buying ceramics cheap, be they shaped in a factory or on a wheel. Abruptly in the late 1960s and early 1970s artistic values were recognized, and almost overnight the jewel-like, hand-burnished, manure-fired creations of certain Rio Grande Valley pottery-makers were selling for thousands of dollars.

To an extent this has already come to Navajo weaving. A large Two Gray Hills of best quality retails for several thousands of dollars.

Compensation for weavers is inadequate, but improving. The economics of a three by five foot vegetal-dye rug at this writing are: from shearing through weaving requires an average of 388 hours. The great time-consumers are carding (40 hours), spinning (90 hours), and weaving (160 hours). If the rug at wholesale sells for $500 the weaver earns $1.30 per hour. As recently as ten years ago a weaving hour might bring only 15 cents.

Says Al Packard, lifelong dealer in Indian arts and crafts in Santa Fe, "If the weaver's income hadn't increased tremendously, there would be few, if any rugs on the market today."

Patrons of San Ildefonso pottery-making do not pay $3,000 for vessels to be used as flower vases. As for weaving, says Packard, "If the rug buyer looks at a Navajo rug simply as a floor covering, he should go to the chain store."

8

A Buyer's Guide to Navajo Weaving

SMALL COMFORT to the casual admirer of the art of Navajo looms, not even men and women who have devoted all their lives to such weavings see eye-to-eye.

One trader who by now has turned over millions of dollars worth of Navajo textiles and judged at the best of shows, tells a story:

"There were four of us judging at a show one year. The scholar among us took a traditional point of view. Our anthropologist was interested in the cultural aspects. We also had with us an authority on raising sheep, and he concentrated on the quality of the wool. My interest was in design.

"And we never agreed on one damned thing."

There exists a market in old rugs as well as new. But rugs are not valuable merely because they are old. Plenty are just bad, old rugs. The buyer of elderly merchandise is well advised to research history and consult a respected dealer before spending hundreds or thousands of dollars for an obviously well-worn and faded item represented as a "classic bayeta," or a "Bosque Redondo transitional" or "a Navajo Moki woven for trade with the Pueblo Indians." Unless documented data accompany such claims, doubt persists. Museum curators confess that unassailable conclusions are difficult to arrive at. Yet at one California auction in 1974 where old weavings were briskly selling in a range $300 to $7,500, the catalog contained numerous errors and misrepresentations — however innocent, one cannot say. The best policy for the buyer of rugs of the past is

76. Some of the most beautiful and unique Navajo weaves are displayed for sale at the Museum of Northern Arizona's annual Navajo Craftsman Show.

97

77. *Helen Kirk*   78. *Grace Henderson Nez*

to become knowledgeable, or hire the services of a professional Navajo rug appraiser. Leads to local appraisers often may be obtained from museums and better shops. Even so, some self-styled appraisers are not experts.

Fortunately, the risk is less for investors in contemporary weaving. Quality and values are more easily established in fresh fabrications. But again, the charm and challenge of Navajo weaves are that no two are alike. Standards are not precise and are further blurred by that intangible element called taste.

One Arizona Indian trader for half a century once took an order for one hundred saddle blankets from a New York riding club. The specifications: the weaves were to be white and nothing but white, all 30 inches square. He enlisted a score of weavers in the project. In three years the blankets were done.

"Few of them were square," he recalls. "The weaves varied, and many were embellished with little designs tucked off in the corners or along the edges. I was almost afraid to ship the blankets, but I did, and luckily the club members were delighted with another example of Navajo individuality."

Several traders pointed out that popularity of certain designs among the buying public cause those designs to be produced most often. But the patterns of taste are capricious. There is no guarantee that the sensation of today will be

79. *Yelthdezbah Davis*   80. *Elizabeth Kirk*

in high esteem tomorrow. A basic resource is to *buy what you like and can enjoy*. That sort of dividend can carry an owner happily across a fluctuation in monetary value.

Some of the guidelines for buying Navajo weaves are those which pertain to all transactions. Deal with dependable, established traders. Get and keep a receipt which describes the merchandise. If today's purchase proves to be less than represented, will the dealer be in business tomorrow? Beyond that:

When assessing a rug, open it fully and lay it out flat. If rugs have been folded and stacked for a long time they may have temporary wrinkles or creases.

Only by seeing a weaving in its entirety on both sides can a buyer be sure there are no serious flaws and that the edges are parallel, straight and square at the corners. The corners should not curl.

Fold it both lengthwise and widthwise to see that opposite sides are at least very nearly the same length. Any substantial variation is a fairly major flaw.

Is the weave the same thickness throughout? Quality work can be heavy or thin, but it's always uniform.

Warp threads should be out of sight. If not, the weaving is seriously flawed. The

81. *Mary Begay*   82. *Betty Shirley*

knowing buyer separates weft threads to determine the type of warp. The presence of warp of cotton twine makes a weave unsuitable for bearing the rough traffic of a floor covering.

No Navajo weaving is perfect. Slight imperfections are acceptable so long as they do not detract from the structural integrity and over-all execution.

Colors should be uniform, especially within design elements. Variations in hue of background areas indicate careless dyeing or carding.

Tightness and consistency of the weave is detected most surely by feel.

Mexican, Oriental and European imitations plague the authentic markets in Navajo weaves. The odor of sheep often is present in Navajo handspun works, and is absent in counterfeits. Of course, the smell of sheep is also lacking in excellent Navajo weaves employing commercial yarns.

Rugs imported from Mexico in recent years, although done in designs suggestive of Navajo weaves, are light to the touch, because lanolin has been removed in cleaning.

The Navajo vertical loom, imparting great tension to the foundation cords during weaving, produces a tightly packed textile. Imitations from Mexico, woven on horizontal looms operated mechanically, are looser of both warp and weft.

Navajo edge warps usually are single, buttressed by edging cords. Mexican edge warps are multiple and generally are not reinforced with edging cords. These clues are not hard and fast. Some Navajo saddle blankets contain doubled edge warps. Imitators are said to be adding edging cords to their copies.

Where to buy?

The Navajo people jealously guard the reputation of their arts and crafts enterprise, based at Window Rock, Arizona, and operating branch shops throughout the reservation.

Tribally sponsored auctions attract bargain-hunters. At places like Crownpoint, New Mexico, auctions are held every couple of months throughout the year. Typically about 200 items are sold each auction day. Other auctions occur at Shiprock, New Mexico, Window Rock and the Heard Museum, Phoenix.

On any day the gift shop at the Heard offers weaving of dependable quality. In Flagstaff a tradition of excellence in Navajo weaving persists at the Museum of Northern Arizona gift shop. Also, a large stock is maintained in the shop of the Denver Museum of Natural History. Splendid examples of weaving are entered for judging and ultimate sale at the annual Navajo show sponsored in midsummer by the Museum of Northern Arizona.

Whatever locale you find yourself in, there are reputable traders in Indian crafts. You can feel comfortable about any rugs purchased from reputable trading posts and shops.

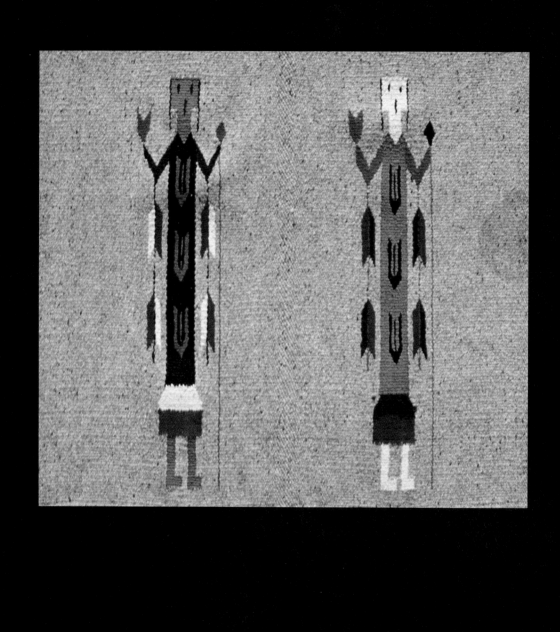

9

Fakes, Frauds and Foolishness

IN 1957 EDITHA L. WATSON in an article in *Arizona Highways* gave reassurance that Navajo weaving was beyond counterfeiting.

"An attempt was once made," she wrote, "to counterfeit Navajo weaving, when an eastern firm tried to promote a line of machine-made 'Navajo' rugs. They might have known what would happen: traders and storekeepers bristled indignantly and refused to even attempt to sell such merchandise. Certainly no one offered to buy it. The firm was forced to call in its samples and write the experiment off as a complete loss."

If once the commerce in Indian goods was so pure, it no longer is today. Concurrent with rising popularity and prices of genuine Indian arts and crafts, the traffic in imitation and fradulent wares has increased also. Hand weaving, long considered invulnerable, today is competing in a world where machine-made imported rugs are foisted off on unsuspecting customers as being of Indian origin.

Sales of Mexican textiles in tourist stores of northern Arizona reached such proportions that the consumer fraud division of the attorney general's office took action. The legislatures of both Arizona and New Mexico made it unlawful to sell such products as Indian made. But problems persist.

A slick national women's magazine advertises, "Navajo. Try an American

83. *This is a detail of a so-called* yei *rug of Mexican origin of a mass-produced type imitating Navajo designs in recent years. It is characterized by multiple cotton edge warps, light, lanolin-free wefts in vivid colors, and reweaving of the ends of the warps back into the weave for an inch or so, 29 x 58 inches.* AUTHOR'S COLLECTION

Indian pattern rug woven of dense, natural yarn in earthtone accents on ivory background or brick reds and golds . . . 4 by 6 feet, $39.95." The ad does not explain that this rug with a copy of a Ganado *pattern,* is imported, from Belgium!

Even when clearly labeled as such, imitation rugs harm the Navajo weavers. As the *Indian Trader* newspaper points out, "It should be noted that much good weaving is done in Mexico. When done honestly in the regional and tribal styles of the weavers it is well worth purchasing. Imitation Navajo rugs, however, sold at prices well below those commanded by authentic Navajo textiles, will only give Navajo weaving unfair competition and undermine the public's confidence."

Particularly handsome is another American-made textile, called the Chimayo, after a village in northern New Mexico. Sixth, seventh and eighth generation weavers of Spanish descent produce serapes and blankets on looms hundreds of years old. These looms are horizontal, are operated by a foot treadle and quickly weave commercial yarn with a flying shuttle. Lovely as they are, Chimayo weaves are no more Navajo than Pendletons.

Not all of the bad business deals are intentional. Traders can't be experts in everything, and some imitations are difficult to tell from the real thing. Nor are

84. *The entire Mexican* yei *rug, a detail of which was shown on page 103.*

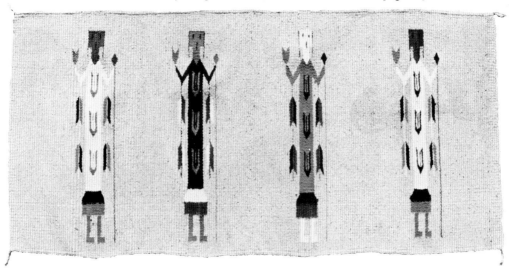

all the villains non-Indians. Some traders claim that Navajos have delivered Mexican imitation rugs to their stores. According to another report, during 1974 some 30 or 40 horizontal, Mexican-type looms were obtained by Navajo weavers on the reservation. If true, this may pose the greatest threat of all to distinctive Navajo weaving. The art might not survive the manufacture of Navajo copies of Mexican imitations of genuine Navajo weaves.

With the rise in monetary value of Navajo weaving and other native arts, an alarming increase in theft and burglary has occurred. Museums, trading posts, city stores and homes of private collectors have been targets of professional criminals. The loot, most of it without identifying marks, is sold through fences from Los Angeles to El Paso, for distribution as far away as Europe. So serious is the increase in crimes related to Indian arts and crafts (a rate of ninety percent per year is one estimate), that in 1974 the Indian Arts and Crafts Association was founded, based at Gallup, New Mexico. Among goals is the registration, by serial number, of valuable items, and a national communications system for alerting dealers, collectors, craftsmen and museums regarding stolen goods.

Another scheme of merit is under consideration by the Navajo Arts and Crafts Enterprises with headquarters at the Navajo capital, Window Rock, Arizona.

Navajo weaving would be authenticated with a piece of metal, stamped with a copyright mark, and permanently wired with a seal to the fabric. As explained by a proponent, "It would identify the store which guarantees it as genuine. It would carry the date of registry and it would have an exclusive serial number. This would be backed up with a detailed history of the item tied into the registry number in protected records so that a buyer could at any time in the future obtain the name of the weaver and other pertinent history."

It's about time.

10

The Care and Feeding of a Navajo Weave

AN ARTISTIC NAVAJO RUG, blanket or wall tapestry will last for generations if given proper care. The inherent ruggedness of Navajo weaving was demonstrated at the Chicago World's Fair when 2.8 million people walked across a rug without wearing it. That was an old-style weave of handspun reservation wool, heavy with lanolin which lubricated the strands against the shock of footsteps. Rugs dating to 1910 survive intact on busy aisles of schools and churches of the Southwest.

The treatment is not recommended for fabrics of recent manufacture. Most modern weaves of wool diminished in oils in refining processes do not have the resiliency of the older rugs. Even *those* proved vulnerable to the peculiar dangers imposed upon a textile spread upon a floor. Dogs gnawed off corners. Cats sharpened their claws. Plumbing leaked. Table and chair legs bored holes. When cocktails, food and coffee were spilled, the rugs were there to catch the outfall. Dirt inevitably was tracked in on shoes. Sunlight streaming through windows unevenly faded colors. Finally, no matter how good the wool or the weave, some wear occurred.

The trend toward moving Navajo textiles from floor to wall solves most of the problems. It creates one that, until the advent of the space age, seemingly had no satisfactory solution. In short, how do you hang a tapestry without hurting it? Nails, tacks and staples are subject to rusting which stains wool. Any system of attachment which distributes weight to a series of fasteners tends in time to cut through strands. The Denver Art Museum curators hit upon a

85. *An award-winning Crystal attractively displayed in a contemporary home.*

method of sewing the top edge of a wall display with clear monofilament (such as fishing leader) to a wooden slat, which in turn is affixed to the wall. While the monofilament is nearly invisible, and weight is evenly carried by the slat, the large stitches impart an unbecoming scallop to the top border.

The ideal alternative grew out of a new system of fabric closure publicized by use in space suits for astronauts. One side of a garment opening would be fitted with a strip consisting of myriad tiny plastic hooks; the other side, a strip of nappy material. Now commonly used in parkas, sports uniforms and swimming suits, the product is marketed under the trade name of Velcro. The type now sold in yardage goods stores usually is less than an inch in width. But wider versions, capable of bearing more weight, are produced by American Velcro Corporation, 681 Fifth Avenue, New York, New York 10022. Particularly convenient is an inch-and-a-half-wide strip of plastic hooks whose back side is pre-coated with contact adhesive protected by a paper shield. In use the Velcro is measured and cut to length, the paper shield is removed from the backing, and the strip of hooks is pressed along a level line at a height where the top of the rug is to be. Once the adhesive has firmly set, the top edge of the weaving is simply pushed onto the hooked strip. Adjustments to even borders and remove kinks are easy. When it's time to turn or clean, the weaving can be pulled off in half a second, no harm done. A Velcro-equipped photographic rack has held hundreds of Navajo blankets and rugs, new and old, and the Velcro strip has acquired only a few stray fibers. One caution: the strip becomes a semi-permanent installation. Removal destroys the Velcro and requires refinishing of the wall. As a courtesy Velcro is sold by the lineal foot to buyers of rugs at Hubbell Trading Post at Ganado.

Here are some other tips for caring for Navajo tapestries:

Never, never shake out dirt. The whipsnap action breaks fibers and loosens the corner knots.

If a rug must go on a floor, use a foam mat underneath to prevent wear and skidding.

Vacuum cleaning is recommended as regular maintenance of floor-displayed rugs.

Moths are persistent and perfidious. Whether placed on floor or wall, wool weavings should be turned at least twice a year. Some experts advise a twice-yearly spray with moth repellant. Others swear by a spring and autumn exposure to a few hours of sunlight.

Navajo wool should never be washed in a machine with soap or detergent and water. Nearly every city of size and some small towns in the Southwest have at least one quality dry cleaners which specializes in Navajo and other native weaves. As often as not lanolin restoration and mothproofing are part of the process.

If water lands on a rug, blot immediately. All aniline dyes will run.

Influenced by warmth and humidity, some of the finer rugs such as Two Gray Hills will shrink slightly and turn up at the corners. The weavers have provided an adjustment: carefully untie the corner knots, making sure to remember how they were tied, loosen the binding cords along the edges, and gently massage some slack into the center of the rug from each corner. Then re-tie the tassels.

For storage, weavings should be mothproofed and rolled on wooden dowels or cardboard tubes. Folding rugs for long periods may inflict lumps and permanent creases.

Even museums and serious collectors sometimes are stumped by the puzzle of what to do with a damaged rug. Broken edge yarns possibly can be repaired by a patient amateur owner, but run dye, faded colors, and internal breaks in weft and warp call for a skill of weaving equal and superior to that of the original. Not many repair persons have the talent and dedication to accept such a challenge.

Museums and collectors may know of local repair experts. Likely they are far behind in orders, despite the high costs for their labors. Some used weaves, as with used cars, are not worth the price of repair. Reputable repair men and women will not take on work which will not result in a finished specimen worthy of repair. In effect this limits repair to tapestries of great intrinsic value, by virtue of rarity, style or execution.

Acknowledgments

IN THE RESEARCH and preparation of this book thanks are due to the San Diego Museum of Man and the Museum of Northern Arizona at Flagstaff, which opened their extensive collections for examination and photography. The courtesies of Stefani Salkeld, Helen Turner and Barton Wright were especially helpful. Gratitude is extended also to Tom E. Kirk, Martin Link, Charles G. Mull, Bill Young and Clay Lockett for their insights into contemporary Navajo weaving. Herb and Dorothy McLaughlin generously provided many photographs from the considerable stock of Arizona Photographic Associates, and where weavings from private collections are pictured, the owners are credited, with thanks. For this book about a native textile, the most important Weaver is one named Paul, whose Northland Press against all odds has established the nation's highest standards of regional printing. For the writer, the unexpected bonus generated in this work is the friendship of James K. Howard, Northland's young editor of *diné*-like patience. A final nod of thanks goes to Robert Jacobson, the designer, for keeping me honest.

Selected Readings

AMSDEN, CHARLES. *Navajo Weaving.* Fourth edition, Glorieta, New Mexico: Rio Grande Press, 1974. Santa Ana, California: The Fine Arts Press, 1934.

BENNETT, NOËL. *Are You Sure?* The Navajo Tribe and The Museum of Navajo Ceremonial Art, Window Rock, Arizona, 1973.

———. *The Weaver's Pathway.* Flagstaff, Arizona: Northland Press, 1973.

BENNETT, NOËL, and BIGHORSE, TIANA. *Working With the Wool.* Flagstaff, Arizona: Northland Press, 1971.

BRYAN, NONABAH G., and YOUNG, STELLA. *Navajo Native Dyes,* No. 2. Education Division, U.S. Bureau of Indian Affairs, Lawrence, Kansas, 1940.

KENT, KATE PECK. *Navajo Weaving.* Heard Museum, Phoenix, Arizona, 1961.

MAXWELL, GILBERT. *Navajo Rugs, Past, Present and Future.* Palm Desert, California: Desert Southwest Publishing, 1963.

MERA, HARRY P. *Navajo Textile Arts.* Laboratory of Anthropology, Santa Fe, New Mexico, 1948.

MERRY, E. S. "So You Want to Buy a Navajo Rug?" Fifth printing, The Inter-Tribal Indian Ceremonial Association, Gallup, New Mexico, 1972.

WHEAT, JOE BEN. "Three Centuries of Navajo Weaving." *Arizona Highways,* July, 1974.

Index

Amsden, Charles Avery, 7
Aniline dye, introduction of, 35
Arthur, Mary, 51

Barboncito, 2
Bayeta, 25–31
Beclabito, 62
Begay, Louise, 50
Begay, Hilda, 62
Begay, Maggie, 50
Begay, Marie, 50
Begay, Mary, 50, 67, 100
Bennett, Noël, 15, 91
Bia, Ella Yazzie, 65
Bighorse, Tiana, 15
Bloomfield, George, 54
Bosque Redondo, 28
Bryan, Nonabah G., 57–58
Burnt Water, 60

Cameron, 65
Canyon de Chelly, 5, 12, 57, 94
Carding wool, 16, 17, 20
Carson, Kit, 2
Cedar Ridge, 65

Chacon, Gov. Fernando de, 10
Chief blanket, first phase, 5
Chief blanket, origin, 29
Chief blanket, second phase, 11
Chief blanket, third phase, 11, 47
Chilchinbito, 65
Chinle style, 57–58
Classic child's shawl, 26
Classic Period, 25–31, 33, 35, 44
Classic serape, 24, 28, 29
Classic serape poncho, 27
Coal Mine Mesa, 66
Cochineal dye, 26
Combs, weaving, 21
Coppermine, 65
Cornfields, 50
Coyote Canyon, 68
Crownpoint auction, 101
Crystal rug, early, 40
Crystal style, 52, 106
Curtis, Sadie, 50

Davies, Ed, 54
Davis, Yelthdezbah, 99

Denver Art Museum, 107
Denver Museum of Natural History, 101
Du Pont dyes, 57
Dyeing wool, 18

Evans, Will, 68
Eye-dazzlers, 34, 39

Fort Sumner, N.M., 2, 28, 31, 33
Four Corners, 1, 62
Foutz, Russell, 38
Fred Harvey Company, 33, 46

Gallup throw, 68, 69
Ganado style, 42, 44–46, 47–51
Gap, The, 65
"General" rug, 44
George, Faye C., 51
Germantown, 32, 34–35, 38
Gilmore, Mary, 57
Gould, Mary Louise, 57

Hale, Blanche, 60
Hardy, Alma, 80

Hatathli, Dr. Ned, 68
Heard Museum, 6, 101
Holiday, Leona, 71
Hubbell, Lorenzo, 37, 46, 48
Hubbell Trading Post, 17, 22, 44, 45, 80, 92, 108

Indian Arts and Crafts Association, 105
Inscription House, 65

Jim, Clara, 50
Joe family, 37–38
Joe, Mary, 57
Jones, Mary Amma, 50
Jumbo, Julia, 57

Kahlenberg, Mary Hunt, 30
Kaibito, 65
Kayenta style, 49–50
Keams Canyon style, 50
Kent, Kate Peck, 50
Kerley's Trading Post, 65
Kirk, Elizabeth, 17, 99
Kirk, Helen, 98
Kirk, Tom, 57
Klagetoh style, 49, 50
Klah, Hosteen, 88

Link, Martin, 8, 12, 25, 44
Lippencott, Bill, 60
Lippencott, Sallie, 60
Long, Patsy, 73
Long Walk, The, 2
Loom, 18, 19
Lower Greasewood, 50
Lukachukai, 71, 72

McSparron, Cozy, 57
Manuelito, Ruby, 90
Many Farms, 57
Massacre Cave, 12, 13

Maxwell, Gilbert, 44, 48
Medicine man, 3
Medicine men and women, 5
Mexican fake, 103, 104
Mexican Water, 64
Mike, Dorothy, 56
"Moki" blanket, 31, 39
Monument Valley, 5
Moore, J. B., 37, 50, 51, 52, 54
Moore, J. B. catalog, 41, 66
Mordants, 58
Mull, Charles G., 27, 28
Museum of Navajo Ceremonial Art, 88
Museum of Northern Arizona, 12, 101
Mute, Elizabeth, 57
Myers, Mabel Burnside, 58, 80

"Natural" weave, 78
Natoni, Mildred, 57
Navajo Arts and Crafts Enterprises, 105
Navajo Community College, 94
Navajo language, 4
Navajo Mountain, 65
Navajo origins, 1
Navajo religion, 88
Navajo Station, 50
Navajo Times, The, 3
Navajo Tribal Council, 4
Navajo Tribal Museum, 5
Navajo weaving, early, 8–9
Nazlini, 57
Nez, Grace Henderson, 50, 98

O'Dell, Mabel, 27

Packard, Al, 95
Paiute Mesa, 65

Pendleton blankets, 33
Pictorial weave, 36, 81, 82, 83, 84, 85, 87
Pine Springs/Burnt Water style, 59, 60
Peshlaki, Ana, 72
"Pound" blanket, 36, 37
Price, Maggie, 60
Pueblo blanket, 9
Pueblo III peoples, 8

"Railroad Blanket," 88
Raised outline weave, 43, 67, 68
Rattlesnake, 68
Red Mesa, 64
Red Rock, 68
Roan, Nellie, 50, 60
Round Rock, 71
Rugs, origin, 35, 36

Saddle blanket, 73, 75, 77
Sandpainting weave, 43, 71, 88, 89, 90
Saxony yarn, 28
Sheep, introduction of, 8
Sheep raising, 15
Sherman, Lt. Gen. William T., 2
Shiprock, N.M., 43, 68, 101
Shirley, Betty, 100
Shonto, 65
Simpson's Trading Post, 88
Slave blanket, 12
Slaves, Navajo, 12
Smith, Agnes, 60
Smith, Ellen, 60
"Spirit Trail," 91
Southwestern Parks and Monuments Association, 46
Spanish intrusion, 2, 8, 26
Spencer, Marjorie, 60

Spider Woman, 7
Spindle, 21
Spinning wool, 16, 17
Standing Rock, 68
Storm pattern, 43–44, 65, 66, 99
Sunrise Springs, 50
Sweetwater, 64

Tanner, Clara Lee, 12
Taugelchee, Daisy, 5, 56
Taugelchee, Priscilla, 57
Teec Nos Pos, 37, 41, 62, 63, 64
Theadore, Julia, 57
Thompson, Lottie, 60
Toadachini, Stella, 50
Toadlena, 52
Tocito, 52
Tohachi, 68
Tom, Mary, 57
Tonalea, 66
Trading posts, 33–35, 37, 46
Transition Period, 31
Tsinnie, Helen, 71

Tsosie, Martha, 68
Tuba City, 65
Twill weave, 23, 72
Two-face weave, 23, 58, 60, 80
Two Gray Hills style, 37, 43, 52, 53, 55, 56, 57–58, 95

Upper Greasewood, 71

Vegetal dyes, 37, 57, 65, 98
Velcro, 108

Watson, Editha L., 103
Weaver's Pathway, The, 91
Weavers, prehistoric, 8
Weaving technique, 18–20, 22, 23
Wedgeweave, 38, 80
Western Reservation, 65
Wetherill, Richard, 88
Wetherill, Wynn, 88
Wheat, Joe Ben, 88
Wheelright, Mary Cabot, 57
Whipple, Esther, 50

White Cone, 50
Wide Ruin, 37, 50, 58, 60, 61
Williams, Esther, 63
Wilson, Audry, 80
Wilson, Elsie, 50
Window Rock, 15, 101
Wool cleaning, 16
Wool shearing, 16, 20
Woman's dress, 30, 31
Woman's wearing blanket, *frontispiece*
Working With the Wool, 15, 19
World War II, 3, 4
Wyman, Leland C., 12

Yabany, Ruth, 64
Yazzie, Annia, 50
Yazzie, Faye, 50
Yazzie, Mary Anne, 74
Yazzie, Philomena, 59, 60
Yei weave, 36, 68, 70, 71, 72
Yeibichai, 36, 71, 72
Young, Bill, 48
Young, John, 48